ANNE FRANK IN THE WORLD

Also by Carol Rittner

The Courage to Care:
Rescuers of Jews During the Holocaust
(ed. with Sondra Myers) 1986

Elie Wiesel: Between Memory and Hope
(ed.) 1990

Memory Offended:
The Auschwitz Convent Controversy
(ed. with John K. Roth) 1991

Different Voices: Women and the Holocaust
(ed. with John K. Roth) 1993

Beyond Hate: Living with Our Differences
(ed. with Eamonn Deane) 1994

From the Unthinkable to the Unavoidable:
American Christian and Jewish Scholars
Encounter the Holocaust
(ed. with John K. Roth) 1997

ANNE FRANK IN THE WORLD

Essays and Reflections

Edited by Carol Rittner

M.E. Sharpe

Armonk, New York • London, England

Library of Congress Cataloging-in-Publication Data

Anne Frank in the world : essays and reflections / edited by Carol Rittner
p. cm.
Includes bibliographical references and index.
ISBN 0–7656–0019–6 (alk. paper).—
ISBN 0–7656–0020–X (pbk. : alk. paper)
1. Frank, Anne, 1929–1945.
2. Jewish children in the Holocaust—Netherlands—Amsterdam.
3. Holocaust, Jewish (1939–1945)—Influence.
I. Rittner, Carol Ann, 1943– .
DS135.N6F7317 1998
940.563′18′092—dc21   97–17605
[B]   CIP
Printed in the United States of America

The paper used in this publication meets the minimum requirements of
American National Standard for Information Sciences—
Permanence of Paper for Printed Library Materials,
ANSI Z 39.48-1984.

BM (c)   10   9   8   7   6   5   4   3   2   1
BM (p)   10   9   8   7   6   5   4   3   2   1

For Janet,
with love

I know that I'm a woman, a woman with inward strength and plenty of courage.

Anne Frank
April 11, 1944

Contents

Introduction   ix
Chronology   xv

Part One
ENCOUNTERS

Victoria J. Barnett: *Reflections on Anne Frank*   3
Albert H. Friedlander: *The Resonance of*
   Anne Frank in Our Time   10
Carol Rittner: *A Fifth Place Behind Fear:*
   An Interview with Helen Lewis   19

Part Two
REFLECTIONS

Dorothee Söelle: *God Was Very Small*
   in Those Times   39
Albert Hunt: *Despair as a Luxury*   49
Patrick Henry: *Mending the World*
   After Auschwitz   58
Leo Goldberger: *Psychological Reflections*
   on Courage   63
John K. Roth: *Can We Move Beyond Hate?*
   Some Reflections on Anne Frank   74

Henry R. Huttenbach: *The Cult of Anne Frank:*
   Returning to Basics   79

Part Three
CHALLENGES

Sidney Bolkosky: *"Voices" of Anne Frank*   87
G. Jan Colijn: *Toward a Proper Legacy*   95
Mary Johnson and Carol Rittner: *Anne Frank*
   in the World: A Study Guide   105

Selected Bibliography, Videography, and
   Teaching Resources   117

Contributors   121

Index   125

Introduction

During the more than fifty years since the end of World War II and the Holocaust—in Professor Yehuda Bauer's words, "the worst man-made catastrophe in history so far"—few stories have achieved the mythic quality of Anne Frank's diary, and few stories have so deeply affected millions of people around the world.

Anne was thirteen when she began writing in her diary on Sunday, June 14, 1942, and fifteen when she wrote her last entry, Tuesday, August 1, 1944, three days before she and her family and others in the Secret Annex at Prinsengracht 263 were arrested by German SS-Sergeant Karl Josef Silberbauer, in full uniform, and at least three armed Dutch members of the Security Police in civilian attire. The inhabitants of the Annex, Anne and her older sister Margot; their parents, Otto and Edith Frank; the van Pels (also known as van Daans) family—Hermann, Auguste, and their son, Peter; and a dentist named Fritz Pfeffer (also known as Albert Dussell) were arrested because they were Jews and in the Nazi worldview unworthy of life.

All except Otto Frank perished in the Holocaust, but for more than two years before that fateful August day, Victor Kugler, Johannes Kleiman, Miep and Jan Gies, and Elizabeth ("Bep") Voskuijl and her father risked their lives to protect the people hidden in those attic rooms. These conspirators of goodness supplied the Franks, the van Pels, and Fritz Pfeffer with food, brought them news of the world from which they had "disappeared," and most important of all, offered them friendship during their months and years of fear and isolation.

What happened that day in 1944 was less dramatic than what has been depicted on stage and screen. There were no screaming sirens or Gestapo cars screeching to a halt in front of the narrow building on Amsterdam's Prinsengracht canal. There were no rifle butts violently pounding against the entrance to the house or on the door behind the office bookcase that concealed the staircase leading to the Secret Annex. The truth is more ordinary. Hardly a neighbor took notice when the small group of frightened Jews were taken away by Silberbauer and his Dutch cohorts. Only the people working in the business office of Otto Frank's old firm were really aware of what was happening to the inhabitants of the Secret Annex. Victor Kugler and Johannes Kleiman were also arrested, but they survived. "Kleiman, because of his poor health, was released on September 18, 1944. . . . Kugler managed to escape his imprisonment on March 28, 1945, when he and his fellow prisoners were being sent to Germany as forced laborers."[1]

Before their defeat by the Allies in 1945, the Nazis managed to kill about 6 million Jews, all victims of the *die endlösung,* the "Final Solution of the Jewish question in Europe"—a Nazi euphemism for the physical extermination of European Jewry. Often I am asked why we should remember the human destructiveness of the Holocaust, why we should encourage students to read and study the diary of Anne Frank. Yehuda Bauer, to whom I referred above, answers that question, I think, when he writes that we must remember that the Nazis were not inhuman beasts, but were perfectly human. That indeed is the problem. If they were inhuman, not like the rest of us, we could just dismiss the whole issue—we are essentially different from them. But that is not true. There were unusual circumstances, to be sure, and an unusual coincidence of factors that led to Nazi atrocities. But the capability of all humans to behave like they did exists, at least potentially. Our task must therefore be to fortify those elements in us that will oppose a development that might lead us into utter immorality. Hence the importance of a learning procedure that will emphasize not only the historical processes, but also the emotional and philosophical side, and make these accessible to the largest numbers possible. That means that the Holocaust must be seen as an extreme point on a line that may lead humanity to self-destruction unless that is prevented.[2]

If SS-Sergeant Karl Josef Silberbauer and his Dutch Nazi collaborators offer one model of human behavior, the people who tried to help the inhabitants of the Secret Annex at Prinsengracht 263 offer another. True, Miep and Jan Gies, Victor Kugler, Johannes Kleiman, Bep Voskuijl and her father were not successful in saving the lives of their Jewish friends, but their behavior demonstrates that there always is an alternative to passive complicity with evil. Such human evidence deserves our attention as much as does evidence to the contrary. Because they are the challenge of the exception, they compel us to ask ourselves why some people, even during the meanest political times and under the most terrible threats of reprisal, act in a morally correct way. Finding an answer to this question demands a double inquiry into the human potential for caring and courage. They remind us as well of what so many people could have done, but what so many did not do.

Anne Frank died in Bergen-Belsen concentration camp, just days before it was liberated by British troops. We cannot recall her or any of the other victims of the Holocaust to life, nor can we undo the wars and crimes of the past. We can, however, pledge to each other that her death and the deaths of 6 million Jews during the Holocaust—and of millions of others caught in the total war waged by the Allies and the Axis powers during World War II—will drive us to greater efforts to engage in the never-ending task of *tikkun olam,* the healing and repair of the world. Perhaps in that way, one of Anne Frank's hopes will be fulfilled. "I want to go on living even after my death," she wrote on Tuesday, April 4, 1944. Live on she does, in her diary, read and reread by millions around the world, and in the work of *tikkun olam* she continues to inspire in so many people.

Anne Frank in the World: Reflections and Essays had its origins in Northern Ireland. In 1993 I helped to bring the "Anne Frank in the World: 1929–1945" exhibition to Thornhill College, a Catholic grammar school for girls in Derry/Londonderry. At the time, I edited a small book, *Beyond the Diary: Anne Frank in the World,* intended to help educators prepare their students for the exhibition. Several of the original essays, slightly adapted, are included in this volume. I am grateful to YES! Publications, Derry, Northern Ireland, for their permission to include the following essays in *Anne Frank in the World: Reflections and Essays:* Albert Friedlander, "The Resonance of Anne Frank in Our Time"; Leo Goldberger, "Psychological Reflections on Courage"; Albert Hunt, "Despair as a Luxury"; Mary Johnson and Carol Rittner, "Anne Frank in the World: A Study Guide"; Carol Rittner, "A Fifth Place Behind Fear: An Interview with Helen Lewis"; and John K. Roth, "Can We Move Beyond Hate? Some Reflections on Anne Frank." In addition, I am grateful to Dorothee Söelle for permission to publish her moving essay, "God Was Very Small in Those Times," which originally appeared in German and is translated for this volume by Victoria J. Barnett.

Each of these authors, as well as the others who contributed to *Anne Frank in the World: Essays and Reflections,* used a different edition of Anne's diary in preparing their contributions for the book. Readers may find this a bit distracting, for which I apologize, but in the several decades since Anne's diary first appeared in English, several different translations and editions have been published. Because I did not ask contributors to use a specific edition of the diary, they each took the liberty of using their favorite one, which accounts for the variations in the quotations used from Anne Frank's diary.

The principal of Thornhill College, Sister Mary Christopher Hegarty, her faculty and staff, encouraged and supported the exhibition at their school. Sister (Dr.) Deirdre Mullan, at the time of the exhibition a member of the Religious Education Department, now its head, did much of the work to organize the educational program complementing the "Anne Frank in the World" exhibition. I am delighted to acknowledge their generous support and once again thank them for all they did to make the project a success.

Anne Frank in the World: Essays and Reflections also includes new essays by scholars, teachers, and writers, both men and women, who think that Anne Frank's diary even today, more than fifty years after her death, has something to say to contemporary readers. I am grateful to each and every one of them for their generosity in preparing contributions for this volume. I also want to thank Peter Coveney, executive editor, M.E. Sharpe Inc., without whose encouragement I would not have taken on another editing and writing task. Esther L. Clark, administrative assistant to Peter, also deserves my profound gratitude for all that she did to bring this volume to completion, as does Eileen Maass, production editor.

Finally, I want to acknowledge and thank Jeanne Elff, one of my students at The Richard Stockton College of New Jersey, who didn't realize when she signed up to do an independent study with me in the Spring 1997 semester that she would get involved in the research and mechanics involved in editing *Anne Frank in the World: Essays and Reflections*. It isn't often a professor can say to a student, "I couldn't have finished it without your help," but, indeed, I could not have done so if Jeanne hadn't helped me. I shall always be grateful to her for her reliability and willingness to do so much more than was required for a grade. I am particularly grateful for the help she gave me with the Chronology and the Selected Bibliography, Videography, and Teaching Resources.

Carol Rittner, R.S.M.
Yom HaShoah, 5757

Notes

1. Afterword in *Anne Frank: The Diary of a Young Girl: The Definitive Edition,* ed. Otto H. Frank and Mirjam Pressler; trans. Susan Massotty (New York: Doubleday, 1995), 338.
2. Yehuda Bauer, "Holocaust Education Is the Key to Preventing Genocide in the Future," *The Press* (Atlantic City, NJ), November 8, 1995, A11.

Chronology

1929

June 12   Anne Frank is born in Frankfurt am Main, Germany.

1929–1932   Unemployment and bitterness in the wake of World War I (1914–1918) lead to great disillusionment with the Weimar Republic and to widespread support for the National Socialist Party (Nazis) in Germany. These are the years of the Great Depression.

1933

January 30   Adolf Hitler becomes chancellor of Germany. The German Jews soon feel the effects of the Nazis' anti-Jewish policies of segregation and forced emigration.

March 20   Dachau concentration camp is established about ten miles northwest of Munich, Germany.

April 1   The Nazis organize a general boycott of all Jewish-owned businesses in Germany.

April 11   In Germany all Jewish public servants are fired.

May 10   The Nazis instigate public burning of books by Jewish authors and other authors opposed to Nazism.

July 14   The Law for the Prevention of Hereditarily Diseased Offspring is passed in Germany.

	Taking effect on January 1, 1934, it orders sterilization to prevent the propagation of *lebensunwertes Leben* (lives unworthy of life). By 1939, some 200,000 to 350,000 persons are sterilized.
September	Otto Frank establishes the Opekta-Works Company in Holland. He looks for a home in Amsterdam.
December 5	Edith and Margot Frank move to Amsterdam.

1934

February	Anne Frank moves to Amsterdam where she begins her Montessori schooling.
September	Pastor André and Madame Magda Trocmé arrive in the mountain village of Le Chambon-sur-Lignon, France to begin their ministry among the Huguenot (Protestant) villagers.

1935

June–August	*Juden Verboten* (No Jews) appears on signs in restaurants and stores all over Germany.
September 15	The Nazi regime decrees the antisemitic Nuremberg Laws. They contain two especially important provisions: (1) The Reich Citizenship Law, and (2) The Law for the Protection of German Blood and Honor. These measures legalize the Nazis' antisemitic policies and provide a legal definition of who is a Jew.

1937

July 16	Buchenwald concentration camp is established.

1938

March 13	*Anschluss:* Nazi Germany annexes Austria.
June 1	Otto Frank establishes a second company, Pectacon B.V.
July 6–15	Representatives from thirty-two nations attend the Evian conference to discuss the German refugee problem. No significant action is taken toward solving it.
September 29–30	Munich Conference parties agree to Nazi Germany's annexation of the Sudeten territories in Czechoslovakia.
November 9–10	Following the assassination of Ernst von Rath, a minor German diplomat in Paris, the Kristallnacht pogrom erupts in Germany and Austria. Instigated by Joseph Goebbels, Nazi minister of propaganda, Nazi thugs burn synagogues, loot Jewish businesses, and beat Jews in the streets of Hitler's Third Reich. Some 30,000 Jews are interned in concentration camps.

1939

January 30	Hitler tells the German Reichstag that another world war will mean "the annihilation of the Jewish race in Europe."
April 7	Jehovah's Witnesses are arrested throughout

	Germany; only those who renounce their faith are released.
September 1	World War II begins with Germany's invasion of Poland. The Germans occupy the western half of the country, including Warsaw, Poland's capital city.
September 2	Stutthof (near Danzig) opens as a detention center for Polish men; it becomes a concentration camp in January 1942.
September 3	France and Great Britain declare war on Germany.
September 27	The Polish army surrenders in Warsaw.
October	Westerbork, an internment and transit camp, opens in northeastern Holland near Assen. The camp was originally built for 750 German Jews who fled into Holland illegally.
November 20	Heinrich Himmler, head of the SS, orders the arrest and incarceration of all Gypsy women, astrologers, and fortune tellers in areas controlled by the Nazis.

1940

January	The first experimental gassing of mental patients occurs in German hospitals. The order for this so-called Euthanasia Program, code-named T-4, was given by Hitler in October 1939 and backdated to September 1. More than 70,000 persons perished before protests, spurred by a few church leaders, brought about the program's official termination on September 1, 1941. In fact, however, the operation continued until the end of World War II.

April–May	Germany invades Denmark and Norway, Netherlands, France, Belgium, and Luxemburg.
April 27	Himmler orders the establishment of a concentration camp at Oswiecim (Auschwitz), Poland.
May 15	Netherlands surrenders to Germany.
June 14	German troops enter Paris.
June 22	France surrenders. Terms of the armistice divide France into two parts: a German–occupied territory in the northwest and an unoccupied territory with a capitol at Vichy.
July 10	Beginning of the Battle of Britain ("the blitz").
October 22	First decree requiring Jewish businesses in Holland to register with the German-occupation authorities and requiring their approval for all business transactions.
December 1	Otto Frank's company moves to Prinsengracht 263, Amsterdam.
Winter 1940–1941	The first refugee, a German Jewish woman, arrives in Le Chambon-sur-Lignon and is welcomed into the Trocmé home by Magda Trocmé.

1941

January 10	A decree is issued in German-occupied Holland ordering all Jews to register with the Census Office. This is in preparation for the deportation of the Dutch Jewish population to concentration camps, which begins in July 1942.
February 12	Following several weeks of Dutch Nazi anti-

Jewish attacks and strong Jewish resistance in Amsterdam, the German occupation government seals the Jewish quarter and decrees that a Jewish Council (*Joodse Raad,* or *Judenrat*) be established in Amsterdam. The Council meets for the first time the next day, February 13.

February 25   As a result of a skirmish on February 12, 400 Jewish men are sent to Mauthausen concentration camp in Austria. In response to the deportation of those 400 Jewish men, a general strike is called by Dutch workers in Amsterdam.

March 1   Himmler orders expansion of the Auschwitz camp; construction of Birkenau (Auschwitz II) begins in October.

March 12   The Nazis initiate the *aryanization* (confiscation) of Jewish property in the Netherlands.

April 29   Dutch Jews are ordered to wear the yellow star.

May 8   Otto Frank's company, Opekta-Works changes its name to Trading Company Gies & Company.

May 9   The Germans order Jewish doctors and dentists in Holland to treat only Jews.

May 15   The Germans dismiss all Jews from government-subsidized orchestras in Holland.

May 27   In Holland, the Germans register all agricultural land owned by Jews.

June 22   Germany attacks the Soviet Union. All of Poland falls under German occupation.

June 25   *Einsatzgruppen* (killing squads) begin mass execution of Jews in the Soviet Union.

June 30   In Holland, the Germans round up 300 young

Jews and deport them to the stone quarries of Mauthausen. None survive the ordeal.

July 31
Nazi leader Herman Göring appoints Reinhard Heydrich to prepare "the Final Solution to the Jewish question."

August 29
Jewish children are prohibited from attending public schools in Holland. Jews are also excluded from Dutch universities.

September 3
The first experimental gassings with *Zyklon B* occur at Auschwitz. Most of the initial 600 victims are Soviet prisoners of war, but about 300 Jews also are gassed.

September 15
The German-occupation government in Holland invokes laws banning Jews from many public places.

December 7
Japan attacks Pearl Harbor. President Roosevelt calls it "a date that will live in infamy."

December 8
The United States and Great Britain declare war on Japan.

December 11
Germany and Italy declare war on the United States; the United States, still neutral in Europe, reciprocates.

1942

January
Hundreds of Dutch-Jewish men are sent to labor camps; orders are issued banning Jews from driving cars and stating that their identity cards must carry the letter "J."

January 20
Under Reinhard Heydrich's direction, the Wannsee conference plans how to annihilate European Jewry. Before the end of

World War II, between 5 and 6 million European Jews lose their lives in the Nazi Final Solution; about 1.3 million Jews perish at Auschwitz.

March 1 — Construction of the Sobibor killing center begins in Poland. Jews are first killed there in early May 1942.

April 29 — The SS Police Leader in Holland issues a decree ordering Dutch Jews to wear the yellow star with a black inscription *Jood* (Jew).

May 5 — Eighty-one Dutch-Jewish political prisoners held as hostages are shot at the Sachsenhausen concentration camp.

June 9–10 — The Czech village of Lidice is destroyed in reprisal for Reinehard Heydrich's assassination. The entire village is leveled; all men over fifteen years of age are shot in groups of ten; the women and children are sent to concentration camps. In all, 199 men are killed; 195 women and 91 children are arrested and deported. All are non-Jews.

June 12 — Anne Frank receives a diary for her thirteenth birthday. Two days later, she begins writing in it.

Also in June — Dutch Jews are forbidden to use telephones.

July 5 — Margot Frank, Anne's sister, receives a notice ordering her to report to the Nazi authorities in Amsterdam, an order that means deportation to Westerbork camp.

July 6 — The Frank family move into their hiding place, the Secret Annex, at Prinsengracht 263, Amsterdam.

July 13 — Hermann and Auguste van Pels and their son,

Peter (the van Daans in Anne's diary) join the Franks in the Prinsengracht hideaway.

July 14   Seven hundred Dutch Jews are seized in Amsterdam; 4,000 others are told to report as labor conscripts.

July 15–16   For the first time, a transport of Dutch Jews, totaling 2,000, is sent from the Westerbork transit camp to Auschwitz.

July 22   The killing center at Treblinka is operational. By August 1943, some 870,000 Jews have perished there.

July–August   During July and August, approximately 11,000 Dutch Jews are taken to the Westerbork transit camp and from there are subsequently transported to Auschwitz.

August 7   Dutch Jews are informed by a special edition of a *Judenrat* newspaper that those who do not immediately register for forced labor in Germany, who do not wear the Jewish star, or who change their residence without permission (that is, go into hiding) will be deported to Mauthausen concentration camp.

September 24   German Foreign Minister von Ribbentrop orders that the Bulgarian, Hungarian, and Danish governments be approached to initiate the deportation of Jews from their countries to camps. The SS and Police Leader in Holland informs Himmler that "the new Dutch police squadrons are performing splendidly as regards the Jewish question and are arresting Jews by the hundreds, day and night."

November 16   Fritz Pfeffer (Albert Dussel in Anne's diary) moves into the Secret Annex.

Late 1942	Himmler orders non-Jewish Poles to be sent from Auschwitz to other camps, while Jews from other camps will be transferred to Auschwitz.

1943

January 11	A transport of 750 Dutch Jews is sent from Westerbork transit camp to the killing center of Sobibor in Poland. During the next three weeks, four more transports with 3,000 Jews depart for Sobibor.
January 18	The Warsaw ghetto uprising breaks out.
January 28	The Nazi regime orders the mobilization of German women for labor service, but the order is never completely implemented.
February 20	Members of the Dutch resistance are executed by the Germans.
February 22	Sophie and Hans Scholl (brother and sister), leaders of the White Rose, an anti-Nazi student resistance movement in Germany, arrested a few days earlier, are tried, sentenced, and beheaded for treason.
February 26	The first transport of Gypsies from Germany arrives at Auschwitz. They are placed in a special Gypsy camp (*Zigeunerlager*), also known as BIIe, in Birkenau.
March 29	An order is issued to deport all Dutch Gypsies to Auschwitz.
Also in March	Jewish patients in hospitals in The Hague and Amsterdam are taken into custody pending deportation.

April	Fifty-five hundred Jews are deported from Holland to Auschwitz. Also, the German occupation authorities order the dismissal of all Dutch officials married to Jews. In addition, an order is issued for sterilization of persons living in mixed marriages.
	Bergen-Belsen is converted from a camp for Soviet POWs—16,000 to 18,000 Soviet POWs died there of starvation and typhus—to a concentration and exchange camp for Jewish prisoners.
April–May	Protest strikes sweep Holland when the Germans order the movement of Dutch POWs to camps inside Germany. An estimated 85 percent of Dutch university students refuse to obey a requirement that they sign a declaration of loyalty to the German occupation authorities.
May 25	Approximately 3,000 Jews are rounded up during raids in the center of Amsterdam.
June 8	A transport with 3,000 children and their mothers leaves Holland for Sobibor. All are gassed on arrival.
June 10	The United Churches of the Netherlands appeals to *Reichkommissar* Artur Seyss-Inquart to stop the "monstrous" and "infamous" practice of sterilizing spouses in mixed marriages with Jewish partners.
June 25	The German foreign ministry representative in Holland reports that 102,000 of the 140,000 Dutch Jews "have been removed from the body of the populace."

Summer	The Gestapo make their only successful raid on a house sheltering Jews in Le Cambon-sur-Lignon. They strike Daniel Trocmé's "House of the Rocks," arresting Daniel and the young Jews who are in his charge and deporting them to Majdanek death camp in Nazi-occupied Poland.
September 3–4	Etty Hillesum, a young Dutch-Jewish woman whose introspective diary and inspiring letters will be acclaimed after the war, is deported from Westerbork to Auschwitz along with her parents and 984 other Jews. Most of these deportees are killed on arrival. Etty Hillesum is sent to the women's barracks and dies in November.
September 25	Rumors circulate in Copenhagen that the Germans are planning an imminent deportation of Denmark's Jews.
September 28	Berlin's final order for the deportation of the Danish Jews reaches German officials in Copenhagen. Georg Duckwitz, a German official, leaks the news to Danish officials. Members of the Danish resistance, politicians, church leaders, and others warn the Jewish community about the German plan.
September 29	At morning prayers, Denmark's Chief Rabbi Marcus Melchior warns members of his synagogue who are told to tell other Jews about their imminent arrest and deportation. Jews go into hiding with their Danish neighbors.
	In Holland, 2,000 Amsterdam Jews are sent to Westerbork transit camp. Only Jews in mixed

marriages and those still in hiding remain in the city.

October 1–2   The Danes begin the rescue of 7,200 Danish Jews. People throughout Denmark, from every social, professional, and economic level, join in the effort to save Danish Jews by smuggling them into neutral Sweden.

October 2–3   Throughout Holland, the families of Jewish men who had been drafted for forced labor are sent to Westerbork internment and transit camp.

October 3   An official letter, issued by the Danish Lutheran bishops to protest the action of the Germans against Jews in Denmark, reminds Danish Christians of their moral obligation to help those in need. The letter is read publicly in every Lutheran church in Denmark.

October 16   A Swedish official reports that 6,670 refugees, 90–95 percent of them Jewish, reached Sweden between October 4 and October 16. Also included in the rescue operation were members of the Danish resistance, and Allied pilots who had bailed out over Denmark (about 40 in all).

November 15   Nearly 1,150 Dutch Jews are deported to Auschwitz, followed the next day by a transport of 995 Jews.

1944

February 10   A transport of more than 1,000 Jews from Westerbork transit camp arrives at Ausch-

March

witz-Birkenau; 800 Jews are gassed while 142 men and 73 women survive selection on the ramp and are assigned to forced labor.

Nazi Germany invades Hungary and begins to subject Hungary's Jewish population (some 825,000 people) to the Final Solution.

April 4

Daniel Trocmé, who had accompanied his Jewish students when they were arrested by the Gestapo, is gassed and cremated at the Majdanek killing center.

May 16

Early in the morning, Dutch SS and police arrest individuals with the characteristics of Gypsies. More than 500 people are imprisoned at Westerbork transit camp; 300 of them are classified as Gypsies, and about 245 individuals are characterized as "asocials." On May 19, 245 of the prisoners are sent to Auschwitz; 30 survive. In late July, 72 male Dutch Gypsy prisoners are transported to Buchenwald, and 35 female Dutch Gypsies are sent to Ravensbruck concentration camp. A total of 16 female and 14 male Gypsies from Holland survive the war.

June 6

D-Day: Allied Forces under the command of General Dwight D. Eisenhower land on the beaches of Normandy, France, to begin the ground battle to liberate Nazi-German occupied Europe.

July 20

Some German army officers attempt to assassinate Hitler.

August 2

The Gypsy family camp in Auschwitz-Birkenau is liquidated.

August 4	Anne Frank and her family are denounced and arrested in their Amsterdam hiding place. They are sent to Westerbork transit camp.
September 3–6	The Franks, the van Pels, and Mr. Pfeffer are deported to Auschwitz death camp together with more than 1,000 other Jews. Mr. van Pels is killed immediately on his arrival in Auschwitz.
September 17	British and American airborne troops jump into Holland as part of "Operation Market Garden."
	Also in September Le Chambon-sur-Lignon is liberated by French troops.
October 7	Revolt by the *sonderkommando* (special command) in Auschwitz-Birkenau; the revolt is crushed by the Germans, but not before Crematorium IV is blown up.
October 28	Anne and Margot Frank are sent from Auschwitz, in Poland, to Bergen-Belsen, in Germany.
November 24	Mrs. van Pels is deported to Bergen-Belsen.
November 26	Hitler orders the destruction of the crematoriums in Auschwitz-Birkenau.
December 20	Mr. Pfeffer dies in Neuengamme, a concentration camp in Germany.

1945

January 6	Mrs. Frank dies in Auschwitz.
January 27	The Red Army liberates Auschwitz; Otto Frank is one of those still remaining in Auschwitz after thousands of prisoners are force-marched west to Germany.

February 13	The fire-bombing of Dresden by the Allies begins; thousands of German civilians die.
March	Anne and Margot die of typhus at Bergen-Belsen, just weeks before it is liberated.
April	Mrs. van Pels dies in Bergen-Belsen.
April 11	Buchenwald concentration camp is liberated by American forces.
April 15	Bergen-Belsen concentration camp is liberated by British forces.
April 30	Hitler commits suicide.
May 5	Peter van Pels dies in Mauthausen.
May 7–8	V-E Day: Nazi Germany surrenders unconditionally to the Allies. The war in Europe is over.
June 3	Otto Frank returns to Amsterdam.
August 6	The Americans drop the first atomic bomb on Hiroshima; 80,000 Japanese civilians die, many instantly.
August 9	The Americans drop a second atomic bomb on Nagasaki; thousands of Japanese civilians die in the firestorm and as a result of radiation poisoning.
August 14	V-J Day: Japan surrenders unconditionally to the Allies. World War II is over.
September 2	The Japanese sign surrender terms on the USS *Missouri* in Tokyo Bay.
November	The Nuremberg Trials of Nazi war criminals begin.

1947

Summer	Anne Frank's diary is published in Dutch under the title *Het Achterhuis* (*The Secret Annex*).

1951   The diary is translated into English.

1980

August 19   Otto Frank dies in Switzerland.

Sources for the Chronology

Fifty Years Ago: Darkness Before Dawn, 1994 Days of Remembrance. Washington, DC: United States Holocaust Memorial Council, 1994.

Fifty Years Ago: From Terror to Systematic Murder: 1991 Days of Remembrance. Washington, DC: United States Holocaust Memorial Council, 1991.

Fifty Years Ago: In the Depths of Darkness, 1992 Days of Remembrance. Washington, DC: United States Holocaust Memorial Council, 1992.

Fifty Years Ago: Revolt amid the Darkness, 1993 Days of Remembrance. Washington, DC: United States Holocaust Memorial Council 1993.

Remembering the Voices that Were Silenced, Days of Remembrance 1990. Washington, DC: United States Holocaust Memorial Council, 1990.

Rittner, Carol, and John K. Roth, eds. *Different Voices: Women and the Holocaust.* New York: Paragon House, 1993.

Part One

Encounters

Reflections on Anne Frank

Victoria J. Barnett

I was introduced to Anne Frank in 1960, when I was ten years old. As I recall, the diary of Anne Frank seemed almost an adventure story. The fact that it was true rendered it more exciting; the fact that it had taken place on another continent and in another era made her story seem impossibly (and safely) remote.

What I remembered from my first reading of the book was not so much its account of Anne's life in hiding and her terrible death, but the impression made on me by her idealism. The sentence I still know by heart is her haunting statement: "I still believe, in spite of everything, that people are truly good at heart." As a child, that was what I wanted to believe and, particularly after I read the diary of Anne Frank, felt committed to believe. Neither I nor the young Jewish girl hiding in Amsterdam knew the fate that awaited her. At the age of ten, I could not imagine it.

That same year, I had another introduction to the Holocaust. My father taught English at a small college, and one of his colleagues was a woman named Georgette Schuler. She smoked cigarettes, dressed in suits, and spoke with a deep accent. Her dark hair was pulled back into a bun, and she wore lots of shiny, dangly jewelry. She was incredibly interesting to me, and she was also one of those rare adults who paid serious attention to children. As a result, I paid serious attention to her, and she is the only colleague of my father's from the period that I can still recall vividly. When I walked into my father's office, she was always friendly, and we would chat while I waited for my father.

One night, I heard my parents speaking in those ominously hushed tones that suggest that something terrible has happened. Indeed, it had: Georgette Schuler had killed herself. It was my first encounter with suicide, and I asked a number of questions. I recall only that my parents told me that Schuler was a refugee from Europe, where such terrible things had happened to her that she could no longer live with the memories.

I do not think that I associated Dr. Schuler's death with that of Anne Frank. The word "Holocaust," of course, was not yet in use. Although I read a great deal and had parents who explained things to me, my ten-year-old notions of history were based on impressions, things overheard or seen in books and magazines—bits and pieces of information that only gradually became part of the whole cloth of knowledge. For most children, history—whether it happened ten years or ten centuries ago—represents another world that seems to have very little to do with this one. The events of that world are far away in the past; they are over. Georgette Schuler's death was my introduction to the concept that history does not end, that the past can intrude on the present, that experience (and the memory of it) can be so terrible as to drive someone to her death years later.

In 1979, I moved to Germany, where I spent the following twelve years. On a cold autumn afternoon during my first year there, I went to Bergen-Belsen, where Anne Frank had died. Bergen-Belsen has an eerie beauty. It is a flat northern landscape, covered with fields of blooming heather that are surrounded by forests of birch and fir trees. The fields are dotted with raised mounds, each marked by a bronze plaque on which numbers are engraved, 5,000, 8,000, 10,000: the estimated number of dead whose remains, or ashes, rest in the soft, sandy earth.

I have heard some people say that Bergen-Belsen is not an adequate memorial to the Holocaust. It is too much like a beautiful cemetery; the simplicity of the mounds and the haunting beauty of the place do not offer a graphic view of what the concentration camps were really like. There is a small exhibition at Bergen-Belsen that does portray the history and reality of the camp. But it is true that Bergen-Belsen *feels* different from the other concentration camps, where many of the original barracks and other structures are still standing. When the British liberated the camp in 1945, typhoid was so widespread that, in the weeks that followed, hundreds of survivors continued to die each day. As soon as they could, the British burned the entire camp, including the hundreds of corpses, to the ground. As a result, visitors cannot walk through narrow wooden barracks or into the gas chamber or crematorium, as they can in Dachau or Auschwitz. What is left is silence, emptiness, the whisper of fir trees, and the broad, pale northern sky.

It is possible, standing amid the purple heather and the birch trees, to feel overwhelming sadness but not horror, and this concerns some people. The Holocaust should be remembered with horror, with outrage, with a burning anger that prevents us from ever shutting the book on this history. Understandably, some people worry that memorials that do not explicitly show what happened offer an anesthetized, more comfortable, less graphic view of history—a history that we can live with.

And there are some who feel that way about Anne Frank's diary. I myself can attest to the fact that a child reading this diary might feel the tragedy of her death without having any idea of what that death really entailed. Although her words are a testament to the anxieties of those who hid from the Nazis, the brutality is still in the background. Her diary ends with the Gestapo's discovery of the hiding place; for what follows, she has left no words.

But the main problem in a contemporary reading of the diary, I think, is that our own lack of innocence makes it virtually impossible to understand the young girl who wrote this book. Everything we know today belies Anne's ingenuous belief in the ultimate goodness of human beings. "I still believe, in spite of everything, that people are truly good at heart." We read these words with different emotions—cynicism? anguish? irony? But the one emotion that is impossible to recapture is the full measure of that young girl's innocence and idealism. We know the reality, which was humiliation, torture, mass graves: a reality so terrible that it continued to drive survivors to their deaths, even years later. It is hard to imagine that Anne, in the final days of her life—shivering and hungry, sick and miserable—could have possessed any remnant of that idealism.

And, therefore, it is hard to imagine that we ourselves have any right to idealism. In the late twentieth century, the

Holocaust has led many of us to abandon this belief in the goodness of other human beings. At best, it seems naive and sentimental; at worst, an affront to the victims. Knowing what we know, who among us could make Anne's statement today, with glowing eyes and a sincere heart?

The focus of many Holocaust scholars has been on the details of evil, for which there is abundant literature and documentation. We are experts in the historical factors—antisemitism, nationalism, mass psychology—that make people hurt others. It is easier for us to understand this than it is to grasp the phenomenon of rescue, or the reality of idealism. Last year, I heard a high school teacher talk about using the 1961 film *Judgment at Nuremberg* in a class on the Holocaust. The biggest problem, he said, was that his students couldn't relate at all to the idealism of the film.

Idealism is passé. We know too much. We know the details of the hell that the Anne Frank who wrote the diary had not yet encountered. Above all, we know that she was taken to this hell and died there. Had she survived, her vibrant spirit might have been broken and defeated. Perhaps she would have ended like Georgette Schuler. Or perhaps her spirit would have triumphed, and her voice would have joined the numerous voices that say, "Never again." But, even in triumph, Anne Frank would have had a different voice, colored by pain, anger, suffering, and the bleak knowledge of what is humanly possible.

But the only voice we have is that of an idealistic girl. Despite everything, I believe it is still important that this voice be heard when we speak about the Holocaust. Part of it, of course, is because only through a close look at individual fates do students begin to grasp the import of what happened in the Holocaust. By getting to know the victims as people with faces, families, histories, and personalities, the full scope of the tragedy becomes more vivid. Even today, the diary of Anne Frank tells an immediate, personal story about what happened to the European Jews that the numbers and statistics cannot convey.

But it does more than that. The diary is timeless because it raises this basic question about human nature: about who we are at heart. In reading Anne Frank's diary, we are reminded of our possibility to be good, of her expectation (and her right to expect) that we be good, of our obligation to reawaken a sense of goodness within ourselves. And, read this way, the diary of Anne Frank is also a radical statement that refuses to allow the Nazi criminals to have the last word. The Nazis tried to wipe out all traces of Judaism, to reduce millions of individuals to numbers, to deprive them of all dignity and identity, and, ultimately, to erase the memory of who they were. With the survival of her diary, Anne has confounded them—not just in her account of the everyday details of a life in hiding, but in the sense of who she was that emerges from every page of the book. Then and now, she embodies the idealism and decency that were so utterly absent from Nazism and remain so lacking in our world today.

As an adult, I can no longer read her statement about the goodness of human beings with a childlike sense of triumph and certainty, but must read it with tears in my eyes. But, even if I cannot feel the same fervor that I did as a child, I believe that Anne's idealism is the key today to understanding part of what happened in the Holocaust. I would like to think that keeping idealism alive is one way of preventing future Holocausts. I only understood the real tragedy of Georgette Schuler's suicide once I had the sense of what had been lost from her world. And I suspect that Otto Frank's decision to publish his murdered child's diary was motivated by his hope that the world would remember Anne, not as part of the ashes in Bergen-Belsen, but as who she was, and was becoming.

The Resonance of Anne Frank in Our Time

Albert H. Friedlander

I meet Anne Frank almost every year. What she says to me does not change in the course of time, even though the new "Critical Edition" prepared by the Netherlands State Institute has her speak in Linear A, B, and C. I am grateful to the dedicated scholars who have prepared this text, which clears up some ambiguities and removes that precious diary from all but the vilest and most obtuse attacks. But, after all, what Anne Frank says to us stands above the translations and transmutations of that moment in time when a young girl clutched a diary to her bosom and wrote on the front end cover: "I hope I shall be able to confide in you completely, as I have never been able to do in anyone before, and I hope you will be a great support and comfort to me" (June 12, 1942).[1]

My postwar friendship with Otto Frank and the times when we walked and talked together—in Amsterdam, London, Paris—gave me new insights into Anne as a person. Yet even during those talks I found myself testing the memories of others with the almost memorized diary. After all, she was entitled to speak for herself, to think for herself. As Anne would write, "I have my opinions, my own ideas and principles. . . . I feel quite independent of anyone."[2] Once, Otto Frank confided to me that he was surprised at the depth of Anne's thinking and religious feelings when he read the diary, since he had tended to think of Margot as the more religious person. And, indeed, Margot's criticism of her father's plan to give Anne a New Testament on Chanukah tends to support the father's impression.[3] But there was the age difference. More than that, there were the constrained circumstances under which they lived, the close supervision by the parents of the children, which both Margot and Anne felt so clearly and resented. In that situation, constant examination leads to withdrawal into oneself on the part of the observed. That they were loved and that they loved rises out of the pages of the diary and continues to be a message to the children and adults who continue to turn to that text; and it must and will survive. But oh!—how we wish that she could have lived and that she could have become the writer she wanted to be.

One of the sad illusions in which we indulge is the "Peter Pan syndrome" in which the object of affection remains eternally youthful. "Would you really want to meet Anne Frank fifty years later?" I have been asked. "Think about it!" And my answer was always: "Yes!" She was entitled to the slow ripening into maturity, the joys and pains even of old age—she was entitled to life, quite apart from the way she has entered into the existence of others. Perhaps her later books might have been disappointing and she would have joined the legion of other authors with one great book against which later works would have been measured and found wanting. What of it? Life is more than a book, even

11

that book, and the reading public can be parasitic in dreadful ways. I think of Otto Frank here. He did not write a book, but he became a legend, and was expected to be a legend rather than a living, growing, changing person. In effect, he was hounded out of Amsterdam because he was no longer the father of the diary, the Otto Frank (read Joseph Schildkraut) of the film and play. He committed the crime of wanting to be himself again, of marrying Fritzi and finding new happiness. But he was strong enough to cling to life, to affirm it and to work within the Anne Frank Foundation in a selfless, dedicated way. One might argue that Anne would not have survived an ungrateful public; but any argument that negates the right to survival cannot be sound. And so, while I talk to the Anne of a thousand nights, I mourn the Anne-that-should-have-been.

And of course, she is the Anne of the Foundation and of the exhibits. When the exhibition "Anne Frank in the World: 1929–1945" first came to London, I worked for it and spoke at the opening. There was criticism: Ken Livingstone, a left-wing radical politician who was often critical of Israel, opened the exhibition, and the Jewish community boycotted it (sometimes, we are extremely stupid as a community) and my wife, Evelyn, and I were among the very few "official Jews" who attended. Yet it gave me the opportunity to meet some of the people who are dedicated to the cause of Anne, and who rightly see the work of the Foundation as that of fighting all prejudice, xenophobia, and racism, which is so much on the rise in Europe and the rest of the world. The exhibition is far more than a presentation of Anne's story: it is a fight against the forces of darkness that overwhelmed the Frank family, European

Jewry, the Sinti-Roma, the homosexuals, and all those who tried to battle against the Nazis in those days.

When the exhibition closed, it had to wait a month for its next venue. Our Westminster Synagogue was delighted and honored by being a storage "depot." Every once in a while, I would wander down to our basement and inspect the large panels and artifacts of the exhibition. Anne was at home in our synagogue in the same house where my family and I live—we live "on top of the shop" in the synagogue—and this was a good feeling for me. Through the years, I have been happy to rejoin the exhibition on various occasions. I participated in the Coventry Cathedral service that welcomed Anne and her message. Canon Paul Oestreicher and I share many tasks and are even contemplating a "joint autobiography." We also share Berlin and Kristallnacht, Selma, Alabama, and Martin Luther King, a concern for the wrongly imprisoned, and therefore much of the spirit of Anne Frank. Here, as for many others in diverse ways, Anne Frank unites those who still believe in humanity and in God.

When I was the Jewish chaplain at Columbia University in New York and, before then, as a rabbi in Pennsylvania, I met Meyer Levin a number of times. He wanted to enlist me in the battle he was waging for his own dramatic version of *The Diary of Anne Frank.* However, I had met Otto Frank in 1957, and was totally convinced of Otto's position. Meyer Levin had much moral and even legal right on his side. Later, I read Meyer's play and found it deeply moving and far more "Jewish" (his own contention). However, without being an impresario or expert on the theater, it did seem to me that Meyer's version would have played to a largely Jewish audience for several months and then would have closed. The play by Frances Goodrich and Albert Hackett, first presented at the Cort Theatre, New York City, on October 5, 1955, called simply *The Diary of Anne Frank,* was one of the great successes on the world's stages and is still being performed almost every year, including a recent, brilliant version presented in Germany. I have always felt it wrong of Otto Frank's lawyers to stop the showing of Meyer Levin's version in Israel. After all, in the early 1990s there was a new version of Anne Frank's diary on British television. It was not that exciting, but it at least showed another generation responding to the story in a way that did no violence to the original. I am told there were compelling legal reasons that forced the lawyers to take action against the Levin play, but I still regret this. The details of the Levin-Frank encounter can be found in the Critical Version.[4] Levin eventually received a small compensation—and the larger compensation of writing a world best-seller with *Compulsion* (1956) and the marvelous novels about the Zionist experience in Israel, *The Settlers* (1972) and *The Harvest* (1978). His novel *The Fanatic* (1963) was a most subjective account of his legal battle with Otto Frank, but it might be argued that his contentiousness was one of the wellsprings for his creativity. In terms of the diary, we should now say that his early championing of Anne Frank's book was an important part of its history, and that it was his love for the diary which motivated him above all else in this difficult situation.

A few years ago, I attended another Anne Frank exhibition. It was held in St. Alban's Cathedral, in the Greater London area, and was extremely well attended and publicized. The night I came, the program included Tippett's *A Child of Our Time* and various selections from the diary, read by a young actress. I read my translation of Paul Celan's *Death Fugue,* various other texts, and talked about Anne Frank. A new London broadcasting station, "Classic FM," had sent a reporter. We sat down after the program and taped a long talk on the importance of Anne Frank in our time. After it was broadcast, a number of persons telephoned me to confirm my own feelings about Anne Frank. She is very much alive in the world of today, particularly among the teenagers responding to the inner battles she records for herself in the diary.

"Can one still write to the Anne Frank house in Amsterdam?" I was asked. I remember how weary Otto could become when he had to answer hundreds and hundreds of letters—and how he would not stop writing until he had answered the very last letter. I do not know who is answering the letters now, except that I am certain that they are still arriving in Amsterdam. And I am also convinced that someone in that building or outside of it is perusing a note from a young girl in Japan or in Paris who wants to know what advice Anne can give her regarding a problem with her parents. Wise and sane answers will be given, and I hope that those who write will be satisfied.

Personally, I still think that the best answers are being given by Anne herself. It is not that the diary is a book of advice to the lovelorn or to those who have problems in their homes. Anne did not give advice. She wrote about herself. She delineated a life under pressure, lived within intolerable barriers that did not permit her to be herself in the way in which she saw herself. Nevertheless, simply by giving an account of herself and to herself, she created a model that can be emulated. The uniqueness of life is shown in the person of a small girl who is forced to grow up overnight: "[A]lthough it may sound pretty mad from an adolescent, I feel more of a person than a child, I feel quite independent of anyone."[5]

These days, children are not permitted to grow up gradually, to explore with caution, to test others, and to make mistakes. In Great Britain not so long ago, two ten-year-old boys kidnapped a baby and killed it—and then looked for another child! A mother left her little child in the home on her own to cope for itself and flew away for a holiday in the sun (the child was found and placed into the care of the court). And many teenagers are told that they will never have a job in the future and that government unemployment benefits are waiting for them when they graduate from school.

It is not the world of the Holocaust; it is the world *after* the Holocaust, filled with a different type of darkness, grown out of those dragon teeth as a bitter harvest. Children still die, in Bosnia, in Somalia, in Rwanda. And the world does not care enough. Perhaps that is one more reason to turn back to *The Diary of Anne Frank*—and to other diaries written by children: Moshe Flinker's diary; Jerzyk Urman's diary. Jerzyk was ten years old when he and his family were arrested. He immediately put poison in his mouth, said, "Daddy, cyan . . ." and fell down dead. The Kripos were shocked and left.[6] Jerzyk's diary was simple and childish at times: "x.11,43 Wednesday: What will happen tomorrow? Pussy came."[7] At other times, we get accurate but involved reports on happenings, and trembling thoughts. It is good to remind ourselves that Anne's diary was not the only report from that hidden world of the children, who saw more clearly than their parents. It is so difficult to accept the fact that more than a million children died during the Holocaust, victims of Hitler's madness. And, once we have realized that every human being is unique, that one child cannot be lost in the multitudes but stands independent, it is impossible for us to cope with the totality. That is why we meet them one by one and say *Kaddish* (the Jewish prayer for the dead) for every child; and that is why our mourning will never cease. *Zachor*! Remember! runs through all our liturgies.

Then, we turn back to Anne Frank, a child standing at the crossroads of time and waiting for us. We mourn her, we rejoice in her, and we love her. And we love the other children as well, and want to remember them in conjunction with Anne Frank. Once, Elie Wiesel and I wrote a liturgy for *Yom Ha-Shoa* (Day of remembrance of the Holocaust), entitled *The Six Days of Destruction, Meditations Towards Hope.* In it, one prayer states:

> The mystery of the En-Sof, of God Who is Near and Who is Far. Who may at times be absent, is always with us. It has been said: "When God's back is towards man, history is Auschwitz" (G. Steiner). Yet in every age there have been those who still reached out to God, the mothers of Israel protecting their children, the fathers pleading with God. The Rav of Slobodka, the girls of the ghetto, the steadfastness of the teachers in the camps is Israel, wrestling with God in the darkness, and prevailing.[8]

Anne Frank is part of that group of those wrestling with

God, fighting darkness, and prevailing. And she must be part of our battles against evil in the days to come.

Notes

1. Anne Frank, *The Diary of a Young Girl: The Critical Edition,* ed. David Barnouw and Gerrold van der Stroom, trans. Arnold J. Pomerans and B.M. Mooyart (New York: Doubleday, 1989), 177.

2. Ibid., 543.

3. See ibid., 412.

4. Ibid., 78–83.

5. Ibid., 543.

6. Jerzyk Urman, *I'm Not Even a Grown-Up: The Diary of Jerzyk Urman,* ed. Anthony Rudolf (London: Mernard Press/King's College, 1991), 7.

7. Ibid., 37.

8. Elie Wiesel and Albert Friedlander, *The Six Days of Destruction, Meditations towards Hope* (New York: Paulist Press, 1988), 70.

A Fifth Place Behind Fear:
An Interview with
Helen Lewis

Carol Rittner

There is no rancor in her of any kind, no hatred,
in spite of everything, no hardening of the soul.
—*A Time to Dance,* BBC-TV

Helen Lewis never met Anne Frank, except through her
diary, and were it not for Anne Frank's diary, I might never
have met Helen Lewis. Allow me to explain. I visit Northern Ireland frequently—sometimes six or seven times a
year—and have been doing so since 1990, when I was
asked by a group of people from Londonderry/Derry to
help organize the 1992 "Beyond Hate" conference.

Because I teach and write about the Holocaust, a colleague of mine—I no longer remember who it was—mentioned to someone in Israel, who spoke to someone in
London, who called me in Scranton, Pennsylvania, where I
was living at the time, and asked if I could help get the
"Anne Frank in the World" exhibition into Northern Ireland. Did I know anyone willing to sponsor and host the

exhibition in an accessible public site? I asked about practical matters, principally, how much it was going to cost.

The practical matters seemed manageable, so I contacted a friend of mine, Sister Deirdre Mullan, a Sister of Mercy and a member of the Religious Education Department at Thornhill College, an all-girls' Catholic grammar school in Derry. When I told her about the "Anne Frank in the World" exhibition, her immediate response was, "Let's do it at Thornhill!" Within a week we were sitting in the principal's office, a project proposal in hand. Sister Christopher, Thornhill College's principal, gave the "go ahead" for the exhibition. During that meeting, I happened to mention there was a Jewish woman living somewhere in Northern Ireland who was a Holocaust survivor and that I wanted to locate her and ask her if she would take part in the educational program Deirdre and I hoped to organize around the "Anne Frank in the World" exhibition. Within a week of my return to the United States, Sister Deirdre excitedly called me. Not only did she have the name of the woman in Northern Ireland who had survived the Holocaust, but she also had her telephone number. Did I want it?

"How did you get it," I asked.

"I heard her interviewed on BBC-radio, Northern Ireland, about a book she had just written, her memoir *A Time to Speak* (Belfast: Blackstaff Press, 1992). I remembered you mentioned something about some woman who survived the Holocaust, so I raced home, called BBC-radio in Belfast, spoke to the interviewer, told him who I was, why I wanted to contact her, and he gave me her home telephone number. Do you want it?"

Did I want it? Of course, I wanted it. "What's her name," I asked.

"Helen Lewis."

Helen Lewis was born into an assimilated Jewish family in Trutnov, Czechoslovakia, now the Czech Republic. She lived through the Nazi frenzy that swept through Europe between 1933 and 1945. Her family was educated, comfortable, and culturally German. She grew up in an atmosphere of mounting tension and antagonism between two world wars, one of which was supposed to make the world safe for democracy, the other to make Europe *judenrein* (Jew-free). *A Time to Speak,* written in elegant and understated prose, is her story.

Unlike Anne Frank, Helen Lewis was not a child when she was sent to Auschwitz, a place Anne also endured. Before Nazi Germany invaded Czechoslovakia, Helen was a newly married young woman, an aspiring dancer. Talented, charming, and beautiful, she had everything to live for, but by the end of World War II, her life was in shambles. She survived Auschwitz, and several other places as well—her left forearm bears the tattoo forever linking her with that place of madness and death—but her mother, her first husband, Paul, his parents, and many of their relatives, friends, and neighbors perished in Auschwitz and elsewhere on the Nazi landscape.

When Anne Frank arrived in Auschwitz in September 1944, she too, no doubt, was tattooed, but we'll never know, because she was murdered by the Nazis in Bergen-Belsen, just before the war ended in May 1945. Helen, more fortunate than Anne, survived Auschwitz and Stutthoff, a concentration camp about twenty miles east of Danzig, near the Baltic Sea. Today Helen Lewis lives in Belfast, Northern Ireland, the mother of two sons, a widow for the second time.

Although Anne Frank and Helen Lewis never met, I think they would have much in common, even beyond their horrific experiences. Both were artistic: one a writer, the other a dancer. Both were hopeful and idealistic. Had she survived, I suspect Anne Frank would remind us, just as Helen Lewis who *did* survive *is* reminding us, that in many places around the world, including the European continent, there once again is an extraordinary savagery of spirit abroad, an increasing and deeply dangerous polarization of ethnic groups. Both, I think, would recognize that what is happening today in places like Bosnia, Croatia, Germany, and the former Soviet Union bears a terrible resemblance to what happened in the late 1920s and 1930s in the Weimar Republic and Nazi Germany when millions of people embraced racism, antisemitism, and xenophobia.

The Holocaust is part of humankind's shared remembrance of failure and the capacity that exists for the destruction of human life and dignity when the bonds of obligation—one human to another—fail. Not long after the publication of *A Time to Speak,* Helen Lewis said in an interview, "In my memory, those who ran the machinery of death during the Holocaust seem like monsters from another world. The sad thing is that if you read the news from all over the world now, you realize they were not so unique." Perhaps, given the chance, Anne Frank might have said the same thing, but we'll never know.

On on a cold and dreary winter evening, in Helen

Lewis's warm and welcoming Belfast home, I had the opportunity to speak to her about her experiences during the Holocaust and to ask her about what she sees happening today.

⌇

Carol Rittner: Do you think it can happen again?

Helen Lewis: Four or five years ago, I would have said "No!" Today I am not so sure. The Nazis used to say that the Jews were filth, vermin, disease, and that the so-called Aryan race had to be purified, cleansed of such filth. To "cleanse" means to eradicate something that is dirty. In what way is "ethnic cleansing" different from what Hitler attempted to do to the Jews? Isn't it the same thing?

Not long ago, I heard some very alarming news about new waves of antisemitism in Eastern Europe. That is very troubling. And somebody wrote and told me that in the Czech Republic someone is reprinting *The Protocols of the Elders of Zion* [an antisemitic myth about a Jewish conspiracy to dominate the world; it is believed to have been written in Czarist Russia in the nineteenth century—Editor's note]. I tell you, I am shocked. It's unbelievable to me that such things could be happening today.

CR: How does that make you feel?

HL: Disappointed, sometimes desperate.

When the war ended, those of us who were still alive thought that evil had been done with once and for all, that it had been defeated. We were idealistic, filled with hope. We thought that from then on there would be one great "brotherhood of man," that East and West, North and South

23

wouldn't exist anymore, except geographically, that we would all embrace one another, that we would all believe in the same God. The ideal world as we dreamed it hasn't come yet. Maybe it still will come, but right now it seems that we are turning backward.

CR: Do you feel despairing?

HL: I am not allowing myself that. What use would it be for me to sit and bury my head in my hands and say, "I am despairing?" What use is that to me, to anyone? It's easy to despair, but I refuse to give in to it. I carry on as best I can. Maybe there's very little I can do, but what I can do I try to do.

Quite frankly, if someone who has been through all *that* was really convinced we were on the way back into the same thing, the only thing left to do would be to take a rope and hang himself, because what happened then [during the Holocaust] is so absolutely, unbelievably dreadful. No one should have to endure such things. If, on the other hand, I don't want to do that, then I have to go ahead and do something positive, something constructive. Perhaps there is very little I can do, but maybe just by living and by behaving normally, by telling people who want to listen— and not everyone does—"Look, it's possible to make a new life again," I can do something against despair.

CR: When you speak to people, especially young people, what do you say to them?

HL: I tell them that so much of what we went through during the Holocaust was based on division and separation of every kind. It started with the Germans separating Jews from everyone else. They made laws that said Jews couldn't go anymore to the theater, or to the cinema. They couldn't swim in the same swimming pools with non-Jews, they couldn't marry non-Jews, or employ them. They couldn't live in the same neighborhoods, and so on. The Nazis kept separating and isolating Jews until finally they went to the extreme: they separated Jews from living by killing them.

The separation taking place in Germany today, where they separate immigrants and put them into hostels by themselves, is such a terrible parallel to what happened in the 1930s and 1940s. The greatest danger is in separation. The only hope lies in bringing people together, in every way, at all levels. This is what I try to say to young people when I speak to them.

CR: Why didn't you leave Czechoslovakia when you saw what was happening in Germany? Didn't you recognize that there was danger for your country as well?

HL: First of all, it was not as simple then as it may seem to you now. Yes, we were aware of what was happening in Germany, but we did not think it could happen to us. Not at all. It was happening across the border, in a different country. Now and then, some of our ethnic German co-citizens became very patriotic in relation to Hitler's Germany, and sometimes that took on slightly alarming forms, but generally, we felt safe. After all, we were living in free, democratic Czechoslovakia. I had a friend who lived in Germany, whom I visited once or twice on my Czech passport, and I had no problem at all.

After I finished high school, my mother and I moved to Prague where I enrolled in Milca Mayerova's School of Dance and also attended the university. Prague was the capital of Czechoslovakia. Prague was Czech in language, culture, everything. There were many Germans living in Prague, but we did not see anymore the ultra-German patriotism of the people in Trutnov. We were never personally affected by antisemitism, although I am sure it existed.

CR: When did you become aware of just how dangerous it was to be a Jew in Europe?

HL: I cannot say exactly, but looking back now, I would say there was a menace on the horizon which perhaps I refused to see. Maybe it was because I was young, and when you are young you think that terrible things cannot happen.

In 1938, shortly after Paul and I were married, Hitler demanded the Sudeten territories in exchange for peace. Our great allies, the British and the French, gave in to him, thinking that by this gesture they had bought "peace in our time." They did, for eleven months, but Czechoslovakia had been sacrificed. Czechoslovakia changed from being a fully democratic, very civilized, advanced country, modeled on Western democracies, into a puppet state of Nazi Germany. In 1939, Czechoslovakia was invaded and occupied. From that moment on, I felt personally in danger, but we stayed.

CR: Why?

HL: In the beginning, it was a bit of inertia. We could have emigrated before the war, but we missed the boat in the truest sense of the word. Later on, when things deteriorated drastically, Paul and I decided we couldn't leave his parents or my widowed mother behind. It would have been impossible for them to go with us, and we just couldn't bear the thought of leaving them behind, so we all stayed.

CR: When the Germans occupied Czechoslovakia, did you immediately feel the full brunt of Nazi persecution?

HL: No. It happened gradually, not in one big blow. I was dancing with my company and, quite soon after the occupation, I was advised to use a different name, a neutral name, just in case someone might say that the director had Jewish dancers in her company. At the time, that didn't seem terribly serious, but then signs went up around the city that said Jews were not allowed to walk in the park, they were not allowed to visit coffee houses anymore, or the cinema. These things may seem minor and unimportant to you, but they are symbols for freedom. That you can go where you want to go is important. To be singled out for *not* being allowed to go where you want to go, that is a warning signal for worse things to come. And they did come. Almost every week.

CR: Did you have to wear the Star of David?

HL: Not right away. First, people lost their jobs, then their bank accounts were confiscated. Shopping hours for Jewish people were limited from three to five o'clock in the afternoon. Goods were in short supply anyway because of the war, so between three and five, there was very little you could get. There was a curfew from eight o'clock in the evening until six or seven o'clock the next morning. Things did not happen all at once; they happened gradually. When the Germans did force us to wear the yellow star in 1941, it was psychologically very, very difficult to come to terms with, because it was meant as a symbol to humiliate us, to brand us as outcasts.

CR: How did your gentile friends react to you, to your situation?

HL: Our Czech gentile friends were wonderful. I can't think of *anybody* who turned us away. Not at all. They visited us; we secretly visited them. We remained in touch. If they had been friends before the occupation, they remained friends after, but at a risk to themselves and us. If anybody had caught them visiting us at night, it would have been very difficult, very unpleasant for them, and for us, too.

CR: Why didn't you go into hiding?

HL: First of all, it was not so easy. Remember, there are at least two people involved: one who hides you and the one who is hiding. None of our Czech friends was in a position to hide us. They were all more or less exposed themselves. Everybody was watched. One of our closest friends—I am still in touch with him—was a former army officer. I am sure the Germans kept an eye on him. There were very few people who were able to hide in Prague. Also, Czechoslovakia had Reinhard Heydrich as *Reichsprotektor.* He was a very brutal man. Before he was assassinated—I prefer to say "executed"—he subjected the population to unspeakable humiliation and hardship. A wrong step, a wrong word, could have been fatal.

CR: When were you arrested and deported?

HL: Again, that did not happen overnight. We were arrested in 1942 and sent to Terezìn, also called Theresienstadt, set up by the Nazis as a model ghetto to fool the world and even the Red Cross. I was there from August 1942 until May 1944. Terezìn was awful, but there is a saying, "The worst that you know is better than the unknown," so we tried to stay there, even though it was terrible.

CR: What was it like in Terezìn?

HL: I was terribly shocked when I arrived there. The first thing that struck me was the incredible mass of people. I was there when the population was at its highest—the summer of

1942—60,000 or 70,000 people in a town which in normal times had accommodated a population of 3,000. I realized immediately that any privacy I may have had before was gone. I was literally never, never going to be on my own anymore. That refers to washing, bathing, lavatories, everything. There were all these people everywhere. There was no way that anyone could sleep in a room by herself. It didn't exist. This was a shock.

There was also the hunger, which didn't hit us right away. On the contrary, when I saw the food, I said, "I will never get used to eating such stuff." I couldn't imagine that one day, quite in the near future, I would be so hungry that I would be glad to get a bite of this moldy stuff. After a fortnight, when what we had in our rucksacks was gone, we began to feel hunger. Persistent hunger not only debilitates your body, but it takes an awful toll on your mind. I would find myself thinking about food a lot, more and more.

Unbelievable as it may seem, there was a cultural life in Terezìn, which at first was forbidden by the Nazis, but later tolerated. In the end, they exploited it because Terezìn served as a "model" camp for Red Cross inspections, and the cultural activities served the Nazis' purposes. It was all done in very primitive conditions, but in some small way it helped the spirit of people, for most people were very unhappy and demoralized. Terezìn was difficult, but later, in light of what followed—we all dreaded the transports, even though we did not know where they went—Terezìn somehow seemed not so bad, and yet it *was* awful.

CR: When were you deported to Auschwitz?

HL: In May 1944. We had known of the existence of a very, very nasty concentration camp called Auschwitz, but the term "extermination camp" we did not know. The journey from Terezìn to Auschwitz was horrible. We were many days and nights in cattle cars, in the most indescribable conditions. When the train stopped and we got out, we were not in a frame of mind in which we could clearly think or feel. You have no idea what this journey was like, but when we saw the gate of Auschwitz, we said, "Oh, God, this is a very bad place." We did not know yet that Auschwitz was the end of the road.

CR: When did you learn "the truth" about Auschwitz?

HL: I was told within the first few minutes by someone I knew, a doctor who had treated me in Terezìn. He told me that the actual purpose of the whole camp was annihilation. He told me in very brief, concrete terms, "Look up at the smoke. Can you smell it? Do you know what it is? It's a crematorium but not a normal crematorium. It burns the bodies of people who were gassed a short time ago." He did not leave me in any doubt that I had arrived at the end of the road. I was so stunned by the horror of it.

We were sent immediately to the so-called Czech family camp in Birkenau [Auschwitz II]. We all went there: old and young, children, everybody. This family camp was a special camp where even children existed—*existed*—for a while. You could see immediately that there was something about it in the air, in the atmosphere, some evil, some dread that you couldn't quite describe. Terezìn had been horrible enough, but being sent out of Terezìn to Auschwitz, we thought we had lost a marvelous, wonderful home.

CR: When you arrived in Auschwitz, were you tattooed immediately?

HL: Almost immediately, the second or third day. It was a psychological blow. The tattoo itself meant nothing. It didn't hurt or anything, but there was a document that we had to sign at the same time as we were tattooed. I found it a bit alarming because in addition to my name and transport number, it said that I was in Auschwitz and that I would be available for special treatment within the next six months. *Sonderbahandlung* was the word. It seemed a strange expression. We didn't know at the time what it meant. I found it very odd that they took us, tattooed us like cattle, and at the same time made us sign a document about our future. Why did they need our signatures if they wanted to kill us?

CR: Did you ever think about God while you were in Auschwitz, or talk to others about God?

HL: Yes, of course, but whatever I say now might not be totally 100 percent the "truth," because I cannot remember clearly enough what I thought about God. Certainly there were moments when we asked ourselves, "How could God—any god—allow this to happen? Where is He now?" There were orthodox people for whom religion and religious rituals had been part of their lives before Auschwitz. They continued to pray in Auschwitz. There were other people who in that situation rejected any thought of a deity. Some people very quickly became corrupted insofar as they thought, "This is an upside down world. This is not normal civilization anymore. Any means to preserve my life and relative well-being is permitted here." I tell you the only way one could manifest any kind of faith was by behaving as decently as one possibly could to those nearest. That was the only way one could remain human and perhaps pleasing to God.

I was actually offered a job in the family camp of Auschwitz which would have put me into a certain authority

31

over a small group of people in the barracks where I stayed. Why it was offered to me I don't know, but I said to the woman, "No, I can't do it. I'm not very good at pushing people around and telling them where to go, what to do, shouting." I got a job in the laundry instead.

CR: It must have been terribly humiliating as a woman, even shameful, to have to pass naked before SS men during the so-called "selections."

HL: You must understand: it is like what you asked me about prayer, God. Normal feelings, normal reactions had ceased. The normal feeling of shame took a fifth place behind fear for your life. You had one thought: if he passes me I'm alive. If he doesn't, I am dead within the next half hour. A normal feeling of shame doesn't enter into it. Maybe for a moment it does, but when you see what is happening to some people, what can happen to some people, what can happen to yourself, well, you do not stop to think about things like shame. Only about staying alive.

CR: How did you cope with getting your monthly period, not having sanitary supplies, and so on? What about women who were pregnant, how did they cope?

HL: I can enlighten you about such things. First of all, the shock on coming into the camp was so great that 95 percent of all women, no matter their age, lost their period right away. I didn't get my period back until much later, after the war, when I returned to Prague. Everybody lost her period. After the war doctors made quite a study of this. From a medical point of view, they were fascinated. As for pregnancy. There were very, very few babies allowed to be born in Terezìn, although there were some young married women who came into Auschwitz who didn't know they were pregnant. This was very dangerous, because if they were discovered, they did not survive. The Nazis wanted to eliminate the Jewish people, so it meant that they were not going to allow a new baby to be born. You can imagine how terrible this was for everyone, especially for the mothers. It was horrible.

CR: Were relationships important in the camps?

HL: Relationships were not only important, they were absolutely, 100 percent essential. You could not stay alone for a moment. For example, when you went to work, and if there was a field, and if you saw some turnips in it—a turnip was a life-saver for a day—one at least, maybe two, had to keep watch, if another person was to jump into the field and quickly grab the turnip. You needed your friend, because as soon as you were isolated, for whatever reason, you were finished.

CR: When were you liberated?

HL: Liberated we were not, at least, not for a long time. First, in early August 1944, some of us were sent to Stutthoff, the brutal labor camp near the Baltic Sea. Conditions were awful, horrible. We had nothing to eat, we were forced to do very harsh work. I ended up with typhoid, but I somehow managed to survive. Then we were evacuated from there at the end of January 1945. The Russian front was approaching rapidly and the Germans thought they [the Russians] might find us. Of course they [the Germans] didn't want that. We were forced on one of those so-called "death marches," forced to walk round and round on those icy roads, with nowhere to go, without any food at all. Weeks and weeks of marching, with rifles and guns aimed at us all the time. It really is a miracle that anyone survived, because if you couldn't walk any longer, the guards just shot you on the spot. Others stepped over you and continued. I managed to escape, not out of any great bravery or courage, but just because I had no choice left. There was very little alternative, really. We had stopped for a moment because the road was choked, and I just jumped into a ditch filled high up with snow. It was the decision of a second. I just jumped off into the ditch and hid in the snow until morning when I crawled into a shed. There were people in a nearby house, who were actually German army soldiers—not SS—I was found by an old woman who lived in the house. The soldiers allowed me to stay the night—actually gave me some food. I stayed with this old woman until the Red Army took over the area.

CR: When did you move to Belfast?

HL: In June 1947 I married Harry Lewis. Harry and I had been friends before the war; he had emigrated to England in 1939, then moved to Northern Ireland and settled in Belfast. He returned after the war. We got married in Prague in 1947. I left Czechoslovakia right after our marriage to take up a new life in Belfast.

CR: Do you suffer from what some people call "posttraumatic stress"? Do those years ever haunt you, have an adverse effect on your life now?

HL: Do you mean am I recalling my experiences every night? I have been very, very lucky. I'm not saying that it hasn't left its effects on me. That would be totally untrue, and in a way, I am what it has made me, but at the same time, I am relatively—*relatively*—un-neurotic about it. Well, I do have one "hangup" and that is that I cannot bring myself, no matter how silly it may seem, to throw out a scrap of food. It happens to me like everybody else that some bread goes moldy. It's not even good enough for the birds, and I have to throw it out, but it costs me an awful lot to do it. I scrape the last bit of food and try to make something out of it rather than throwing it out.

I will tell you one other thing: I used to have persistent nightmares. Always the same. It would happen about once a fortnight. I would wake up screaming. Harry would have to put all the lights on. I couldn't sleep for the rest of the night. That happened at regular intervals. But from the moment my first son was born, I never, never had any of those nightmares anymore. Oh, I have normal nightmares, like the ones you have, but never those nightmares. My interpretation is that life defeated death. Giving life, defeated death.

⌒

Helen Lewis not only opened the "Anne Frank in the World" exhibition at Thornhill College in April 1993 with a moving presentation about Anne Frank's diary and her own experiences during the Holocaust, but she also generously choreographed an excerpt from Anne's diary, working with a small group of Catholic and Protestant young people who performed it at the opening ceremony for the exhibition. Nearly 3,000 people—Catholics and Protestants—came to view the exhibition in Thornhill College's spacious sports hall where it was housed for two weeks. They learned about Anne Frank and her diary, and about racism, bigotry, and xenophobia today. As Helen Lewis remarked to me, "Now if we in Northern Ireland can only learn to live with each other peacefully."

Peacefully, indeed.

Part Two

Reflections

God Was Very Small in Those Times

Dorothee Söelle

Just over fifty years ago, on January 27, 1945, Auschwitz was liberated. This date of reflection and (so I would wish) of collective national mourning has a subjective, biographical significance for me. The experience of the *Shoah* runs like a leitmotif through my attempt to reformulate Christian faith. In my well-read copy of the diary of the Jewish girl from Amsterdam, Anne Frank, one place is underlined. On October 9, 1942, she writes: "Nice people, the Germans! To think that I was once one of them too! No, Hitler took away our nationality long ago. In fact, Germans and Jews are the greatest enemies in the world."[1]

How often have I wished that Hitler had made me stateless as well! That I didn't belong! Anne Frank may distinguish between Germans and others, and that attests to her ability to make distinctions and express herself clearly. But, for me as a German, it is not so simple. Ultimately, everyone who didn't resist was involved, bound up in the various forms of co-belief, cooperation, and co-profit. And to these "fellow travelers," in the truest sense of the word, belong all those who practiced the art of looking away, not listening and remaining silent. There have been many disputes about collective guilt and responsibility. But my fundamental feeling is one of ineradicable shame: to belong to this people, to speak the language of the concentration camp guards, to sing these songs that were also sung in the Hitler Youth and the League of German Maidens. This shame doesn't subside; indeed, it must remain alive.

I understood collective shame when, after the war, I visited Holland, the host country of Anne Frank. There, I encountered people who didn't want to talk to Germans. A passerby turned away when I asked her in German for directions. She could see that I was too young to have played an active role in a Nazi organization, but that was irrelevant to her. The shame was in me, and the external humiliation added to it.

I spent almost ten years of my young adult life with the question of my generation: How could that happen? What did my parents do against it? On which side did my teachers stand? What traditions of my country prepared the way for "that," as we always said? Was Luther involved, Wagner, Nietzsche? Or Heidegger? Weren't the schools like soldiers' barracks? The families there to produce serfs? Where were you when "it" happened, we asked the adults. For years, basically, we did nothing else but pose these questions. We were like Oskar, the drummer in Gunter Grass's *The Tin Drum.* Who wanted to be an adult and belong to the masterminds or murderers, the spies or torturers, the railway officials or nurses who were involved?

The worst reply to our numerous questions was the denial of reality, such as: "We didn't know anything about it. We didn't have any contact with Jews. In our village there was nothing 'like that.' We heard bad things about concentration camps, but they were just for criminals and homosexuals. And for Jews too, yes." These answers, heard in a thousand places, made the shame even more impossible to evade. Sometimes, helplessly, I replied: "Have you read Anne Frank's diary?"

I wanted to know exactly when, where, in what way, by whom, the Jews had been murdered. Today, when I encounter someone from my generation who doesn't know what *Zyklon B* is, I become nervous. Later, I tried to develop a post-Auschwitz theology—not one before or beyond this event. I didn't want to write a single sentence in which the knowledge of this, the truly greatest catastrophe of my people, is not present or cannot be made present.

How did I arrive at this position? All that I learned that was enlightening politically, all which gradually led me out of the dull fog of a tragic, irrational Germanness, did not come from institutions such as the church, schools, or political parties. I learned in my family's home, from eyewitnesses, returned emigrants, refugees, survivors. Soon after its appearance, I read Eugen Kogon's *The SS-State,* and, slowly, the darkness of a romantic, cultivated, bourgeois German youth lightened.

Only late did I enter a process of reappraisal, which turned out to be lifelong, born of my deep feeling of shame. Collective shame is the minimum that a people with a history like that of the Germans needs. At the same time, it contains a transformative, progressive momentum. As one of the great German philosophers said, shame is "a revolutionary act."

As a young teacher during the Adenauer era, I soon established that German history in my school stopped with 1914. German fascism didn't appear in the lesson. Some of the teachers were directly affected and didn't want to know, the others had never learned about it and didn't know how to handle it. In any case, they took the easy way out and hushed everything up.

One day, I used the example of the Nazis to explain something to my fourteen-year-old students. A week later, the children came into class and said, "My father said the Nazis weren't that bad, they built the Autobahn." With that, I noticed that not only my class but the students in the entire school knew absolutely nothing about the Nazi era. This was the reality of the 1950s.

Independently, together with a colleague and close friend, I drafted a lesson plan for the seventh to twelfth grades to teach about National Socialism. We were relatively free to develop our religion lessons. When there were objections, we told the people in the church bureaucracy that, for pedagogical reasons, we couldn't do it any differently, and we soothed the state officials by saying that our procedures were theologically indispensable. Having to serve two different masters has its advantages.

I recall a very gifted class of fourteen-year-olds in which we discussed the Nazi era. They served up their parents' rationalizations: Hitler took the unemployed off the streets, got rid of inflation, restored order, and so on. By coincidence, I had eighteen girls in my religion class. In my desperation to make something clear, I had them stand up and count off in groups of three. "Imagine," I said, "that all those who said three have to leave. They are sent to be gassed. There were 18 million Jews in Europe before Hitler." Later, this method appeared pedagogically problematic to me; but it wouldn't be forgotten.

My first step toward theology was connected, politically and historically, to a feeling, of which I was not conscious at the time, that the liberal Protestantism and German culture of my family, where one sooner read Goethe than the Bible, had been helpless and unable to prevent 1933. Nor could they prevent anything after 1939. And they were naive in 1945, when they thought: now we can start anew from where we were before.

In my teaching years, I learned to ask: Why did the German bourgeoisie overturn, and betray its liberal thoughts and ideas? How could parents and teachers assume that the bourgeois culture, which found its definitive end in Auschwitz, could be rescued through rebuilding, reeducation, rearmament, and restoration of the old patterns of ownership and everything else? Were the Nazis only a nightmare for them from which they awakened, and not the consequence of this German history? How could they hope to start over "again" without a radical break?

I found the bourgeois cultural relationship to Christianity too cool and indecisive; nothing else had replaced this legacy. That wasn't serious enough for me. What drew me to Christianity was its deep respect for each individual life: You can save your life or lose it. When people remain in this apathy, this prepolitical consciousness of the three famous monkeys who hear nothing, see nothing and, above all, don't want to protest, then this is a destruction of human dignity.

The development of the Federal Republic confirmed my mistrust. At my first major public appearance at the

Kirchentag in Cologne in 1965, I made a statement that brought me immense difficulties. It was: "I don't know how, after Auschwitz, one should praise the God who gloriously reigns over all."

Two fundamental theological questions had changed for me: the question of sin and the question of God's omnipotence. Today, the phrase "political theology" almost belongs to church history. My book, *Political Theology—A Debate with Rudolf Bultmann,* appeared in 1971. It grew out of the experiences that our group, "Political Prayer Evenings," had had in Cologne since 1968, out of experiences in light of the Vietnam War, and the effect this war had upon us and the student movement. The book is a reflection of the theoretical background of our praxis at the end of the 1960s. In response to the book, Bultmann wrote me a four-page-long critical letter; I would like to cite one passage from it here:

> I agree with you that through certain changes in the social structure, the number of constraints that today force us to sin could be reduced: but what does it mean to sin? According to my "individualistic" understanding, there can be no talk of sin that is caused through the constraints of the social structure. I understand sin as an offense from person to person, that is, for example, as a lie, breaking of trust, temptations and such things, but not as a collective transgression against the commandments. You are correct in your intentions. But that which you characterize as sin, I call guilt. You make no distinction between sin and guilt. To exemplify on your example of bananas: there is indeed a distinction between whether I murder a banana grower or whether I receive bananas through the United Fruit Company. If the banana grower is too poorly paid by this company, he can always take the legal route or strike.

I had to laugh about this, but also to weep. The greatness of liberal thought is its hope, and this hope represents a part of the legacy to which we must hold firm. This hope is absolutely naive and has not the slightest access to reality because this banana grower, this *campesino,* this exploited slave can neither go on strike nor take legal measures. Liberal thought appears here as utterly unreal, but, at the same time, it contains a standard that one can never, under any circumstances, do without.

The difference between guilt and sin cannot be expressed in such a way that guilt is the collective and sin only the individual. I hold that to be an utterly false division, particularly from my experience and reflection about the fate of our people, the German question, and what it means to be a German after Auschwitz. I can say with one word what distinguishes me from Bultmann: Auschwitz. My attempt to pursue theology is shaped by the consciousness of living after Auschwitz. In contrast, Bultmann thinks along the lines of a bourgeois understanding of scholarship as above the times and objectifying.

One of the consequences of this is precisely that this concerns sin, and that, in view of 6 million murdered Jews, we cannot dissociate ourselves from personal sin. My consciousness of sin rests on the collective things that happen in my country, in my city, in my group. I would like to say openly that the individual sins with which I reproach myself and that, naturally, I notice in my life, nonetheless take up far less space. That is simply my experience. What I suffer under, that for which I pray for forgiveness, where I need forgiveness—those are the catastrophic things that we as a society today do to the poorest and to our mother, the earth.

For this, in order to make clear at all what this is about, I need a language that reaches beyond the education that is necessary—a language other than that of explanation, definition, and critique. That is the point where, I believe, I try to go farther than Bultmann, not back to a biblical naiveté or into a preenlightened world, but, after the passage through the Enlightenment, into a new language. This new language is what we seek, what we are working on, in liberation theology.

Long after my studies, I got to know the Jewish writer Elie Wiesel. He told me how he treated his son, who at that time was about eight years old. Every evening, father and son had an established hour together. Wiesel said that for that reason he didn't like to travel and, when possible, took his son with him. There were a few rules for this time together. Each of them could ask anything; each tried to reply as best as he knew. The boy, for example, asked his father to tell about his school days. "How was it when you were a boy?" He asked about the teachers, the schoolmates. The father told him a great deal. Then the boy sometimes asked questions like, "Where is your friend now?" Or: "Is the teacher still alive? What happened then? Does the cherry tree still stand in your uncle's garden?" And the father didn't answer. He said nothing. He was silent. And one day the boy asked his father a strange question. He said: "Was that before or after?" The father had told the child nothing about deportation, about extermination camps, about gas. And still the boy knew something and referred to it with the words "before" and "after." "That was before, father, wasn't it?" he said. At some point the father will have told him what happened between before and after.

When, in 1946, 1 heard the "St. Matthew's Passion" for the first time again, the powerful chorale "His blood will be upon us and upon our children" had been left out. What was possible "before," had become impossible "after." The event had stained the words, the thoughts and pictures, and given them another meaning.

Nothing makes my aging so clear to me as the impossibility of conveying to my descendants what Auschwitz has meant for my generation. Naturally, I try. Naturally, I find it outrageous when people who can explain the quantum theory don't know words like *selection, ramp, Zyklon B*. Naturally, I have asked myself again and again: how can we pass on the history of disgrace? And, still, I sense the gap between the generations. How can I hand down the feeling of shame and disgrace so that they will not be forgotten? How can a national identity originate that doesn't "work through" this, our past, but passes it on?

I struggle against my own aging, it's true, against my own experience becoming one that is discarded. But also against the announcement by anyone in my country that "we are somebody again," in which I hear the clear rejection of the feeling of collective shame.

Auschwitz didn't end in Auschwitz. "What can we do?" I asked Elie Wiesel. The Jewish tradition teaches that we should pray and do justice. No one should come and supposedly not have known about it. It means not to let everything happen to one, but to resist. It means to give bread, not ever more refined weapons, to the hungry. Prayer means not to despair. Prayer is a contradiction of death. It means to collect oneself, to reflect, to win clarity about what we live for, what we want with our lives; to have a memory and, in that, to be more like God; to have wishes for ourselves and our children; to express those wishes loudly and softly, together and alone, and, through that, to become ever more like the human beings we were meant to be.

Through these theological changes, it has become ever more clear to me that the picture of the heavenly sovereign, omnipotently enthroned in heaven, who allowed events like the *Shoah* to happen, has changed. "Power in relationship" is something other than an almighty lordly power that depends upon no one.

God was very small in that era that lies a little more than fifty years behind us. His sun did not shine. Her spirit had no dwelling among us. He had few friends. Perhaps only the mystical language that speaks not "about" God, but to her, is in the position to name this God who needs us. As Jakob Bohme put it, God is "the nothingness that wants to become all."

Translated by Victoria Barnett

Note

1. Anne Frank, *The Diary of a Young Girl: The Critical Edition,* ed. David Barnouw and Gerrold van der Stroom; trans. Arnold J. Pomerans and B.M. Mooyart (New York: Doubleday, 1989), 274.

Despair as a Luxury

Albert Hunt

My son, Chris, rang me from Hiroshima to wish me a happy
St. Valentine's Eve. He's teaching English in Hiroshima.
Hiroshima is the place where the Western Allies dropped a
bomb in August 1945 that killed more than 80,000 people.
The Western Allies were the Good Guys. They were fight-
ing the Good War against unimaginable evil.

Chris rang me from Hiroshima on St. Valentine's Eve
because it was on St. Valentine's Eve 1945 that RAF
Bomber Command set fire to Dresden. For many years a
group of us from Bradford had commemorated the bombing of Dresden in a play we'd invented called *A Carnival
for St. Valentine's Eve*. Dresden was bombed on the night
of Shrove Tuesday, carnival night. Children were roaming
the streets in carnival clothes—it must have been a bit like
Halloween.

We performed our play on several St. Valentine's Eves
and took it eventually to Dresden. Then a group of Dresden
students adapted it and performed it there on St.
Valentine's Eve in 1984. I went to Dresden in what was
then East Germany to see it and afterward walked with the
students across the vast firestorm area. One of them tried to
light a candle outside the carefully preserved ruins of a

church. East German police came out of the shadows and threatened to arrest him. The candle was put out and the police went away.

I thought I'd finished then with Dresden, but a few years later I was given the opportunity by BBC–Channel 4 to make a documentary, not just about Dresden, but about the bombing of cities in Europe. In the documentary we talked to a navigator who had helped to bomb Dresden and to a friend of mine, Erika Woollams, who survived the fire-storm and now lives in London. Chris worked with me on that program. So he rang me from one violated city to remind me of another.

Oddly enough, I hadn't been thinking about Dresden at all. I'd been thinking about this essay, about my Jewish friend Maria Lewitt, who has lived for forty-five years in Melbourne, but who survived the Nazi occupation of Po-land because she had blonde hair and blue eyes. About how warm it is in February in Melbourne, about meals I'd eaten there in the open air on soft St. Valentine's Eves. And about the England cricket team in India, and the latest Burnley football results.

But after Chris rang, I took a glass of wine into the gar-den—to my mind, one of Christianity's better ideas is to drink wine in remembrance—and sat on the doorstep. Marker flares were dropped over Dresden at six minutes past ten and the first bombs were falling by thirteen minutes past. Eighteen minutes later, this first of three attacks was over and the city was on fire. So, on this mild February night, I sat in the garden by myself with my glass of wine, for the eighteen minutes of the raid, and thought about the schoolgirl friends Erika Woollams had shown me in a photograph—all of them had died in the raid—about Erika herself escaping to the river bank, with the firestorm raging behind her, about her being machine-gunned the following day by low-flying American fighters, about the people who had jumped into an emergency water tank and had been boiled alive, about the ones who had been found dead from lack of oxygen in shelters that had been opened in the weeks after the raids— *corpse-mines,* Kurt Vonnegut was to call them in *Slaughterhouse Five.* And I thought, too, about the little hill I'd seen on the edge of another German town, Pforzheim, a small town known as the Gateway to the Black Forest, burned and bombed ten days after Dresden.

I'd first heard of Pforzheim while I was making the TV documentary. Out of a population of 83,000, 17,800 people had been killed in a forty-five-minute raid. The navigator I interviewed who helped to bomb Dresden had helped to bomb Pforzheim too—in his log book he noted that he'd seen another bomber blown up in front of his eyes during the raid. He'd no idea that there had been a firestorm and that so many people had been killed—but, as he said, Pforzheim was a military target; they were making telescopic sights for the U-boat fleet that no longer existed in February 1945, only weeks before the end of the war.

There was nowhere to bury the bodies in Pforzheim, so they took them to the edge of town and piled them up into what became this little hill—it's covered with grass now and looks just like a natural hill. So I thought about the hill, and about the other sixty German cities burned by the Allied bombers, and about the half million or more dead German civilians, and the 53,000 air crew members of Bomber Command, who died doing what they believed was necessary in the Good War against unimaginable evil, and the German fighter crews who died trying to protect the cities—I met some of their survivors too. And then I found myself thinking about Majdanek.

Majdanek didn't exist before the war. But in that summer of 1989, when I was editing the bombed cities documentary, I found myself in Lublin, an old city in southeast Poland, not far from what was then still the Soviet border. Miraculously, the old city center had survived the war, but high-rise blocks have been built on the Polish plain, and from the train the city looks like a colony on the moon. An Irish friend of mine, Aidan Doyle, from Cork, who teaches the Irish language to Polish students in the Catholic University of Lublin—I'm not kidding, he really does—lived in one of the high-rise blocks, and he took me down to the nearest bus stop and a bus came along that had MAJDANEK on its destination indicator.

Majdanek was a Nazi death camp a few miles down the road from Lublin. I got Aidan to take me on a kind of pilgrimage—in the same way that I'd made pilgrimages to the Warsaw Ghetto, to Buchenwald, and to Anne Frank's house in Amsterdam. You are shown the gas chambers at Majdanek, and huts with piles of clothes and shoes belonging to the inmates who died there. But at the entrance to the camp there was an exhibition of anti-Nazi propaganda. Before the Nazi terror had come to Majdanek, said the exhibition, it had struck in Western Europe. There were huge photographs of the results of Nazi terror bombing in Rotterdam, Coventry, London. Only—and remember I was working with documentary material on the bombed cities—I recognized, or thought I recognized, that the photograph of the huge area of devastation labeled London was in fact a photograph of Hamburg.

Hamburg was destroyed in a week of raids at the end of July and the beginning of August 1943. Fifty-three thousand civilians were killed—more than the total number in Britain in the whole of the war—and the first man-made firestorm was created. In a firestorm a lot of little fires come together to form a great whirlwind of flame. People and objects are sucked into the blaze. That's what happened in Hamburg and Dresden and Pforzheim and Hiroshima and Nagasaki and many other cities in World War II. All the firestorms were created by the Good Guys in their fight against unimaginable evil.

As I walked around Majdanek, where Polish farmers were piling up fresh-smelling new-mown hay and Polish boys, on a school trip, were chasing and wrestling each other, I thought about the photograph of Hamburg that was labeled London, and looked at the pitiful piles of shoes, described as having been worn by the inmates, and thought irreverently that they could have been collected from anywhere and wondered if that thought was making me look at them differently. A friend of mine called Hajo Hermann—I think of him as a friend—the most unlikely people become friends when you talk to them. In the "Beyond Hate: Living with Our Deepest Differences" conference, held in Derry, Northern Ireland, in September 1992, I sat next to Reagan's ambassador to Dublin and even she behaved like a friend— so: a friend of mine called Hajo Hermann, who bombed with the Condor Legion on the wrong side in the Spanish Civil War, and who bombed Warsaw and probably bombed my wife in Liverpool, and who later became a

53

fighter pilot and spent ten years in a Soviet prison camp, and is now a lawyer in Dusseldorf—Hajo Hermann, when I last heard from him, was defending a man who was on trial in Germany for trying to prove, using forensic evidence—where have I heard that one before?—that there never were gas chambers at Majdanek, only showers where inmates were deloused (it's illegal to say this in Germany).

I like the way revisionists use the word "only." I've read books that say the Holocaust never happened, that "only" half a million and not 6 million Jews died in camps. RAF apologists for Dresden say that "only" 35,000 were killed there, with 35,000 missing, and not 400,000, or even 120,000, as was once thought to be the case. The other night I saw an Israeli military spokesman on television who said that "only" 30 to 40 people died in the massacres in the Sabra and Shatila camps in Lebanon in 1982—who asks us to remember those any longer?—and not 2,000 to 3,000, as many witnesses claim.

I'm afraid, Hajo, that I believe in the gas chambers at Majdanek, in spite of the photograph of Hamburg that was labeled London. I'm with George Orwell on war atrocities—I believe they happen even though the *Daily Telegraph* says they do. And I believe in the wine of remembrance—which is why I'm glad we're being asked to remember Anne Frank. But—again to paraphrase Orwell—I'm uncomfortably aware that while all memories are equal, some are more equal than others. And that all of us have a natural tendency to indulge those memories that confirm our own sense of moral rightness and to consign the others to the oblivion holes of history.

When we went to Pforzheim, we were told that we were

the first British visitors anybody could remember showing an interest in the bombing. We were welcomed by the deputy mayor because the mayor was visiting Guernica. Guernica was bombed by the Condor Legion in the Spanish Civil War. The mayor of Pforzheim was trying to set up an association of bombed cities, bringing together Guernica, Warsaw, Rotterdam, London, Coventry, Berlin, Cologne, Hamburg, Dresden—the list could be endless. The deputy mayor offered us any help we needed in making our documentary, in the hope that it would help to make sure that no other Pforzheims ever happened.

Less than two years later, in January 1991, I came down to breakfast to hear on BBC radio that the bombing of Iraq had begun and that 19,000 tons of bombs had been dropped in the first hours. And I remembered that it had taken only 2,800 tons of bombs to wipe out Dresden. I wondered what on earth the 19,000 tons was supposed to be hitting. And in the weeks that followed, as the bombs rained down on Iraq, I raged in futile despair that all the efforts of historians and witnesses to make the bombing of populations as unacceptable as the Nazi death camps had apparently changed nothing.

Which brings me at last to the supposed subject of these random recollections. It's good to drink the wine of remembrance. But when we drink it simply to confirm the sense of our own rightness, we give ourselves the right to rage against the unimaginable evil of those we think of as enemies. Only when the rage doesn't destroy the evil, it quickly turns to despair. "When will they ever learn?" asked Bob Dylan in his protest song about the young men who were "gone to soldiers every one." The implied answer is, "Never!" Nearly half a century after World War II, bombing returns to Iraq. And ethnic cleansing returns to Europe. And what can any of us do except drink the wine of remembrance and wring our hands in despair?

Well, we can stop enjoying our despair for a start! And start using our wits, intelligence, imagination, and sense of mischief to invent a new script for ourselves and our situation, a script that, as my friend Eamonn Deane puts it, isn't a victim script.

Ivana Balen, who came to the "Beyond Hate" Conference from Belgrade, told one of my favorite stories of 1992. In Belgrade, she works with a women's resistance group that helps young Serbian men to evade the draft. And she told how a friend on the ground floor of a block of high-rise flats rang a young man who lived on the top floor and warned him that the Serbian military were coming up in the lift to deliver his draft papers. So he hurried out of his own door, locked it, and was knocking at the door when the conscripters arrived. There was, of course, no reply from inside. So he raged about himself to the men with the draft papers: "That crafty bugger! He owes me money! He'll have buggered off out of Belgrade! I don't suppose I'll ever see him again." After which, the women's group spirited the young man out of the city and away from the clutches of the army.

It's not the kind of story that makes it into high-sounding news bulletins about the war. But it is the kind of response to apparently desperate circumstances that gives your spirit a lift and invites you to drink a toast to wit and invention instead of remembering in despair.

When I was making the documentary about the bombed cities, I came to respect the men who had flown over Germany in the crusade against what they saw as unimaginable evil. Again and again they told me that they did what seemed right at the time.

But the stories I really enjoyed include the one about the man who crashed his Wellington in training and succeeded in never dropping any bombs at all. And the one about the man I met in Dusseldorf who, with a friend, broke into the block warden's room, borrowed an official stamp and forged Hitler Youth papers, which they used to avoid going to Hitler Youth meetings. If they were ever stopped by inquisitive authorities, they always had the right papers. This man was called up toward the end of the war and promptly volunteered to join a parachute regiment. He calculated that by the time he finished his special training the war would be over. When he was sent anyway to the Western Front, he succeeded almost immediately in being captured by the Americans. He and a friend were busy when I met them trying to get a monument erected in Bonn to those who deserted from the German army during the war.

So, a toast, by all means, in remembrance. Of Anne Frank and of the others who ask to be remembered. Of the schoolgirl friends of Erika Woollams who were burned alive in Dresden. Of the 80,000 killed in Hiroshima. Of the 30 or 40 or 2,000 or 3,000 Palestinians who were massacred in the Sabra and Shatila camps. Of . . . but you can fill in your own names.

Drink up. But take your empties to the bottle bank for recycling. There's a lot of enjoyable, inventive, and imaginative living to do.

Mending the World After Auschwitz

Patrick Henry

*I want to be useful . . . I want to go on living
even after my death.*

—Anne Frank

Rereading Anne's diary fifty-two years after her death provides illuminating insights into our world as well as hers. It would be possible to offer contemporary commentary on dozens of passages whose significance still resonates at this crucial moment in our collective lives when there will soon be no one among us with any memories of the Holocaust.

Anne's sense of shame, "I can only stand by and watch while other people suffer and die";[1] unworthiness, "[God has] given me so much, which I don't deserve";[2] and even guilt, "I feel wicked sleeping in a warm bed, while somewhere out there my dearest friends are dropping from exhaustion or being knocked to the ground"[3] constitute a veritable leitmotif in her confessions to Kitty, one that can be heard just as poignantly in the writings of survivors publishing their memoirs today.

58

Her November 19, 1942 entry, that continues the introduction of the new boarder in the Secret Annex, Mr.
Dussel, contains this important observation: "I'm not exactly delighted at having a stranger use my things, but you
have to make sacrifices for a good cause, and I'm glad I can
make this small one. 'If we can save even one of our
friends, the rest doesn't matter,' said Father, and he's absolutely right."[4] Not only does this passage give us insight
into Jewish rescuers of Jews, but it allows us to shatter the
myth of Jewish passivity (which always ends up blaming
Jews for what happened to them) by, among other things,
redefining heroic activities Jews were involved in—saving
other Jews, for example, most often their own children.
Anne's diary reminds us how little we still know about
Jewish resistance and Jewish rescuers of Jews.

More central to Anne herself and to her particular personality, however, is the striking observation made in her
May 3, 1944, entry: "There's a destructive urge in people,
the urge to rage, murder and kill. And until all of humanity,
without exception, undergoes a metamorphosis, wars will
continue to be waged, and everything that has been carefully built up, cultivated and grown will be cut down and
destroyed, only to start all over again."[5]

Anne's unvanquished optimism—"I cling to [my ideals]
because I still believe, in spite of everything, that people
are truly good at heart"[6]—allowed her to espouse the possibility of that transformation of humanity toward the good,
and calls to mind Daniel Trocmé, a Christian rescuer of
Jews in the village of Le Chambon-sur-Lignon in south
central France. Daniel, a professor of language, history, and
geography, was responsible for two houses where Jews

were hidden. Although he could have easily escaped during a Gestapo raid in the summer of 1943, he remained with his charges and was arrested with eighteen refugees. He died, approximately ten months before Anne, on April 2, 1944, in a gas chamber at the Nazi extermination camp Majdanek in Poland. In a letter to his parents a year before his arrest, he explained that "Le Chambon is something of a contribution to the reconstruction of our world."[7]

It is precisely the metamorphosis of humanity hoped for by Anne and the reconstruction of our world begun by Daniel that face our post-Holocaust generation. The question to which we must respond is not the excruciatingly unknowable: "What would I have done had I lived in occupied Europe?" but the more urgently concrete: "What can we do now to help build a world where another Auschwitz would be unthinkable?" In attempting this monumental endeavor, we do at least have a model to work with—the rescuers of Jews during the Holocaust. These courageous persons, although only a fraction of the 700 million people who lived in Nazi-occupied countries during World War II, were part of the picture. Indeed, these lights that shone only here and there in the overall darkness enable us to see and to find our way out of the labyrinth of blind hatred in which they lived. Who, then, were these people, and how might we begin to populate the world with such beings?

The findings of Gay Block and Malka Drucker, who interviewed 105 rescuers from eleven different countries,[8] and of Eva Fogelman and her staff, who interviewed over 300 rescuers and the Jews they rescued,[9] are similar. On the whole, neither gender, nor age, nor nationality, nor educa-

tion, nor profession, nor economic class, nor religious lean-
ing, nor political persuasion played a determining role as to
who would be a rescuer. Whereas most people surrender
personal responsibility for their actions when those actions
are dictated by an authority figure,[10] the rescuers of Jews
obviously did not. Why not? Block, Drucker, and Fogelman
would say because, as children, in the great majority of
cases, they were raised in homes where love was in abun-
dance, where parents were altruistic and tolerant, and where
children were disciplined by reason and explanation. In
these homes they were taught five essential principles:
human beings are basically the same and differences between them are to be respected; the world is not divided
into "us and them" but rather contains a common bond of
humanity; they should have a clear sense of right and
wrong, should stand up for their beliefs, have moral integrity, self-confidence, and self-worth; kindness and compas-
sion toward others should be practiced; and they should
have an independent mind, be self-sustaining, and never
follow the crowd.

How are we to respond to Anne and Daniel, whose stubborn faith in humanity speaks out to us so vividly fifty
years after their horrific deaths? What will we do today to
bring forth new life from their ashes? In their memory and
in the memory of all those who were subjected to the Holocaust, the victims who died and those other victims, the
survivors, do we really have any other choice but to emu-
late and embody, as parents, teachers, and simply as human
beings, the values of those who, rising to their defense,
performed at the summit of human potential?

Notes

1. *Anne Frank: The Diary of a Young Girl: The Definitive Edition,* ed. Otto H. Frank and Mirjam Pressler; trans. Susan Massotty (New York: Doubleday, 1995), 149.

2. Ibid., 157.

3. Ibid., 73.

4. Ibid., 71–72.

5. Ibid., 280–281.

6. Ibid., 332.

7. Pierre Sauvage, *Weapons of the Spirit* (Los Angeles: Friends of Le Chambon, 1987). See also Philip Hallie, *Lest Innocent Blood Be Shed: The Story of the Village of Le Chambon and How Goodness Happened There* (New York: Harper & Row, 1994), 205–217.

8. Gay Block and Malka Drucker, eds., *Rescuers: Portraits of Moral Courage in the Holocaust* (New York: Holmes & Meier, 1992).

9. Eva Fogelman, *Conscience and Courage. Rescuers of Jews during the Holocaust* (New York: Doubleday, 1994).

10. As we know from the Milgram experiments. See Stanley Milgram, *Obedience to Authority: An Experimental View* (New York: Harper & Row, 1974).

Psychological Reflections on Courage

Leo Goldberger

As a youngster, I grew up in German-occupied Denmark where I personally witnessed acts of heroic courage. Mine is the story of how I, along with some 7,000 Jews, was saved from the claws of the Nazis by our neighbors and friends—spontaneous acts of thousands of ordinary Danes during the darkest days of the Holocaust. They exemplify a group of people who individually and collectively are honored as "righteous gentiles" and from whom we can all learn a moral lesson as we confront the mess we are in today all over the globe.

Observations from Psychology

Bravery and courage come in many forms, ranging the gamut from the magnificent feat of St. George confronting an awesome dragon or King David sparring with the giant bully, Goliath, to the quite seemingly ordinary—for example, the unarmed, solitary Chinese student we saw on our TV screens a few years ago, placing himself in front of an oncoming tank during the Tiananmen Square demonstra-

63

tions. Courage is revealed in many disparate behaviors but is by no means limited to overt actions as such. For example, the attitude of hope in the face of adversity—illness, war, injustice, and hatred. Does that not bespeak of bravery and courage? Anne Frank clearly typifies this point.

Anne Frank was a budding adolescent, idealistic and eager to experience and enjoy life to its fullest. She was also a Jew and thus, during the Nazi era, a victim of irrational hate and persecution. She was forced into hiding, as incomprehensible as it must have seemed to her, cooped up in the cramped space of an attic, living day by day in an atmosphere fraught with danger and despair. Although she and her family would ultimately get caught and be put to death in Bergen-Belsen concentration camp, she never wavered in her attitude of optimism and hope. She never stopped coping the best she could under her tragic circumstances. Shortly before her arrest she wrote in her diary:

> It's really a wonder that I haven't dropped all my ideals, because they seem so absurd and impossible to carry out. Yet I keep them, because in spite of everything I still believe that people are really good at heart. I simply can't build up my hopes on a foundation consisting of confusion, misery, and death. I see the world gradually being turned into a wilderness. I hear the ever approaching thunder, which will destroy us too. I can feel the suffering of millions and yet, if I look up into the heavens, I think that it will all come right, that this cruelty too will end, and that peace and tranquillity will return again.
>
> In the meantime, I must uphold my ideals, for perhaps the time will come when I shall be able to carry them out.[1]

Anne Frank has become a symbol of courage, not just for

adolescents, who can readily identify with her as they go through their own growing pains and fears, but for all of us.

The example of Anne Frank's courage suggests that psychological abstractions such as "attitudes" and "feelings," subjective and hidden from view though they be (revealed perhaps only in a personal diary), can convey the most admirable and civilized of human qualities. The dictionary defines courage as "the state or quality of mind or spirit that enables one to face danger, fear or vicissitudes (read anger or hate, as one such vicissitude!) with self-possession, confidence and resolution." Perhaps no one has said it better than Aristotle in his general discussion on moral virtues. For him courage was achievable in the balance between two vices, one of excess and one of deficit. The person who exceeds in confidence is rash; whereas the person who exceeds in fear is deficient in confidence and is cowardly.

Aristotle's wise observations are readily translatable into modern-day psychology. What Aristotle is saying is that our basic emotions—fear, anger, and hate—derived as they are from our animal heritage, are instinctively or automatically triggered, often to the extremes. Our basic emotions prepare us for the task of fight or flight. Obviously anybody can feel fear, anger, or hate. To avoid a dangerous situation altogether, or alternately, to fight, to take revenge on another person, is no great human achievement. These basic emotions and response patterns are never lost. They persist as evolutionary vestiges, serving a vital function when sheer survival is at stake. But it is only when these archaic patterns of behavior can be energetically tamed, transformed, or modified by rational, realistic, and situational considerations that we can speak of a genuine human achievement. It is then that we can speak of behavior that is civilized, or, in Aristotle's words, "conduct that is noble and praiseworthy." This is where the process of learning comes in, which involves parental nurturance, worthy role models, and meaningful efforts by educational and religious institutions. It is a life-long process, never fully successful, since there's always the potential for flare-ups of our instinctive response patterns.

The fight-flight mechanism often gains full sway in circumstances that present no threat whatsoever to biological survival, at least not in any rational or realistic sense. In our daily lives, "threats" come into play when psychological rather then physical integrity is at issue; when economic and interpersonal security is at risk; when a person's identity (personal, national, or religious) is undermined; when vanity, pride, status, and a host of other human vulnerabilities suffer severe blows. In short, situations in which one's sense of equilibrium and status quo is upset.

If one couples the fight-flight mechanism with yet other innate psychological mechanisms, for example, displacement and projection, which frequently come into play inappropriately, one can account for much of the evil in the world. The most common example of displacement is to be found in the man who feels rage toward his boss, avoids expressing it, but abuses his dog instead. The familiar notion of scapegoating is yet another example in which displacement and projection are at work. A person may feel insecure or inferior about something in himself or herself and by simply blaming or accusing somebody else—usually someone of another race or religion—the pain of having to confront oneself and perhaps do something constructive about it may be temporarily eased. These maneuvers are especially venomous as they generally take hold of attitudes and behaviors totally outside the person's awareness and control. Forceful external, educational efforts are required to root them out.

Fortunately, there are many self-reflective, noble, and praiseworthy individuals whose psychological well-being does not depend on the pathological use of displacement and projection. These are the people who habitually act with courage. They are the "hardy" people. The "hardy" person may be said to be a person who embodies the following three characteristics: (1) a sense of commitment to a set of moral/ethical values and to whatever he or she undertakes; (2) a realistic sense of personal empowerment; (3) a way of coping with stressful situations, including life-threatening illness such as cancer or AIDS, by viewing them as "challenges" to be overcome by realistic problem solving, or at least by maintaining hope. Conversely, the nonhardy person views most stressful situations not as challenges but as threats to be submitted to, fought blindly, or simply denied or escaped from, be it by alcohol, drugs, or other forms of displacement. Research shows that "hardiness" is associated with physical health and speedier recovery from illness as well as with optimism, sense of humor, and a predilection for love over hate. No doubt, were Anne Frank given the "Hardiness Test Questionnaire" she would pass with flying colors. We don't know how many "hardy" persons there are in any given population or culture, but ultimately the challenge is to figure out how to enable more people to become "hardy" souls. Research shows that it can be done through education and therapy.

Denmark During the Holocaust

From my own experience, I want to recount briefly the courageous behavior of Danes who came to the aid of Jews during the Nazi occupation of Denmark by putting their own lives on the line. The Danes, truly, became their Jewish brothers' and sisters' keepers. Events in Denmark during 1943 exemplify not only courage but also altruism on a massive scale. In an age of self-centered narcissism, these events are especially worthy of recall.

When World War II began, Denmark, with a population of some 4.5 million people (and an air force of a mere thirteen planes!), declared its neutrality. She even signed a nonaggression pact with her big neighbor to the south, Nazi Germany. Nevertheless, in a surprise move during the night of April 9, 1940, Denmark was invaded. There was some token resistance, but the Danes were simply overpowered. The five-year-long occupation by the Germans began. Some 7,800 Jews (including 1,500 children of mixed marriages) lived there, many of whom had lived there for generations, with full civil rights and religious freedom. The Jews were no different from other Danes except for their religious faith. There were no ghettos and hardly a whisper of antisemitism. And no amount of German pressure on the Danish government could alter this situation, at least not during the first three years of the occupation. Thus, despite our anxiety about the Germans all around us, and having heard how they treated Jews elsewhere in Europe, we continued to live our normal lives as Jews the best we could, attending our parochial schools and synagogues and participating in our community activities. Increasingly, however, more and more opposition and tension developed between the Danes and their German occupiers.

By the summer of 1943, the Germans were getting fed up with the increasing number of violent acts of resistance, bomb attacks on their rail supply lines, and the reluctance of local factories to cooperate with them. Sterner measures were needed, but the Danes resisted. In late August the government, which had tried to be as accommodating as possible toward the Germans (on the condition that they were left in charge of domestic issues, including the fate of their Jews), simply quit. King Christian X resigned and was placed under house arrest. The Germans were furious. They retaliated brutally all around. They declared martial law and instituted a strict curfew. The Germans unleashed their hatred, not only toward members of the Danish resistance movement but also toward the Jews. Finally, the Germans began implementing the Final Solution. They planned to arrest the Jews during Rosh Hashanah (the Jewish New Year) in 1943, the night between October 1 and 2, when they would all be at home. A courageous German official leaked the word of the round-up to a few Danish politicians, who in turn warned the Jewish leadership, barely three days before. The warning spread quickly, and most Jews went into hiding immediately. Every Dane who learned what was happening helped, despite the danger to themselves if they were caught. Without hesitation they hid the Jews in their homes; they arranged escape routes across the sound to Sweden; they drove Jews to fishing villages, small inns, deserted factories where they waited until the coast was clear for their escape. Doctors and nurses helped hide fictitiously named Jewish patients, transporting them via ambulances past Gestapo guards to the coast. Fishermen all along the coast were pressed into service, concealing Jews in cargo bays, eluding the German patrols. Within a two-week period, 7,200 Jews were saved in this manner. There were some mishaps and tragedies—about 50 drowned—and some were so distraught they committed suicide rather than risk getting caught. Some 460 were caught and sent to Theresienstadt concentration camp in Czechoslovakia. Most of them survived because the Danes, through the Red Cross, monitored their fate and sent them food parcels even while they were in the camp.

I was only thirteen when all this happened. Oddly enough, what I remember most clearly are the moments of excruciating fear intermingled with moments of courage. Two emotions that are, of course, intermeshed in response to danger. First there's the fear; then if one succeeds in overcoming it, there's courage. One example may suffice: My experience of fear was at its maximum when I awoke one night, in late August of 1943, and heard some loud knocks on our door, with Germans yelling "Open Up!" (The Germans had come to take my father, a cantor in the synagogue, as a hostage, along with other officials in the Jewish community.) My father tiptoed into my room and whispered, "Keep very quiet. We'll pretend no one's here." As the pounding of the gun butts continued, my fear increased. I remember pleading with my father to open the door. I thought the Gestapo would break it down any minute and in a rage shoot us on the spot. But my father, assessing the total situation realistically, did not make a move. (In hindsight, I would say he acted courageously!) An upstairs neighbor insisted that the Germans stop the

70

racket they were making in the middle of the night, and then matter-of-factly told them that the Goldbergers were not at home.

Though our upstairs neighbor's act was relatively minor in the scheme of things, he showed what could be called "goodwill," perhaps the first step toward courage. As we began a month-long period of agony, hiding in various places and trying to make the necessary contacts to escape to Sweden, I again saw the intermingling of fear and courage—almost on a daily basis. But, miraculously, courage won out. We found so many ordinary Danes willing to help us, willing to take risks. It was not just that they were willing, they felt it was their natural duty to help us in our hour of need. For the people who helped us, it was a matter of simple human decency. It did not involve a deliberate decision-making process; it was behavior that was experienced as flowing spontaneously, congruent with the person's total being and sense of self.

For example, a typical Danish "rescuer," when asked after the war why he or she helped the Jews, said: "It was the only thing I could do, to help a fellow human being, whether Jew or not." Similar remarks were made by other rescuers from across Europe. A French rescuer: "We were just people trying to do our best." A Dutch rescuer: "It did not occur to me to do anything other than I did. . . . We all have memories of times we should have done something and didn't. And it gets in your way the rest of your life."[2]

Much has been written about the righteous gentiles—those who helped save Jews during the Holocaust. Obviously the Danes qualify, as do the people who helped Anne Frank and her family, even though their efforts were not successful. The fact that "rescuers" are a widely disparate group, and the acts they performed of such widely different nature and magnitude, makes it almost impossible to derive a personality profile of them. But were one to pursue the question in a psychologically sophisticated manner, "hardiness," rather than the narrower trait of "altruism," surfaces as the core feature, as can be seen in the earlier cited comments by typical rescuers.

But clearly, acts of courage must also be viewed within the context of specific historical and situational circumstances, and within the social norms at a given time and place. For example, the circumstances in Holland under which Anne Frank and her family lived were far different from the situation that prevailed in Denmark. The German occupation of Holland was much more severe. There was no obvious escape hatch for the 140,000 Jews living there—other than going into hiding as the Franks did, at least for a while. The special restrictive laws for the Dutch Jews were implemented in gradual stages, leading ultimately to social isolation, beginning with the wearing of the yellow Star of David. The Jew, in essence, became an "untouchable," a person to be shunned. The acts of courage needed under these circumstances, which involved being in opposition to the prevailing laws and social norms, involved far greater risk than in Denmark. For the Dutch it might have involved that "extra special something," which unfortunately made courage fairly scarce.

It is that "extra special something" that is sorely needed again to help overcome the evils of yet another of our powerful archaic vestiges—the herd instinct. In its adaptive form the herd instinct fosters social units and a sense of mutuality that constitute the very foundation of culture and the enrichment of our individual lives. But in its pathological form, it emerges as cruel tribalism, ugly exclusionary nationalism and, God help us—ethnic cleansing! Having endured and survived the Holocaust, how can civilized human beings ever fathom its repetition?

Notes

1. Anne Frank, *Anne Frank: The Diary of a Young Girl,* trans. B.M. Mooyaart (New York: Pocket Books, 1958), 237.

2. See Carol Rittner and Sondra Myers, eds. *The Courage to Care: Rescuers of Jews During the Holocaust* (New York: New York University Press, 1986), passim.

Can We Move Beyond Hate? Some Reflections on Anne Frank

John K. Roth

> *That's the difficulty in these times: ideals, dreams, and cherished hopes rise within us, only to meet the horrible truth and be shattered.*
>
> —Anne Frank

Every Monday morning I receive an electronic mail transmittal called *The Irish Emigrant*. This digest of Irish news is produced by a man named Liam Ferrie. Each week he collects news from all around the island and dispatches it by e-mail to some 1,500 readers all around the world.

I began to read Ferrie's weekly summaries a few months before I first visited Derry, Northern Ireland, in February 1992, to participate in an important year-long project, "Beyond Hate: Living with Our Deepest Differences." *The Irish Emigrant* remarked favorably on that international conference, which occurred in Derry in September 1992. More recently, however, Ferrie's news about Derry has included some somber notes. For example, his dispatch on April 14, 1997, mentioned that four days earlier a member of the IRA (Irish Republican Army) shot Alice Collins, a forty-six-year-old RUC (Royal Ulster Constabulary) policewoman and the mother of three children, as she stood on duty outside the Derry City Courthouse on Bishop Street.

Although I write these words thousands of miles away from the spot, I can see that Derry location very clearly in my mind's eye. As I do so, the words quoted above from *The Diary of Anne Frank* are also on my mind. They raise again questions that are not only Derry's or Ireland's but everyone's everywhere: Can we live with—and not kill and die over—our deepest differences? Can we find ways beyond hate?

Consider those questions by observing that a twenty-one-year-old law student, Horst Wessel, died in Berlin on February 23, 1930. He was caught in "sectarian violence" that would soon escalate to become "ethnic cleansing" and then the Holocaust.

The Nazis had another name for the Holocaust, or the *Shoah,* as it is often called in Hebrew. They called it the "Final Solution." The name fitted: the Holocaust was Nazi Germany's planned total destruction of the Jewish people and the actual murder of nearly 6 million of them. That genocidal campaign—the most systematic, bureaucratic, and unrelenting ever—also destroyed millions of non-Jewish civilians because the Nazis believed their threat to the Third Reich approached, though it could not equal, that posed by the Jews.

Like many other young men in the Germany of his day, Horst Wessel, a Lutheran pastor's son, rebelled against his

75

bourgeois upbringing and joined the *Sturmabteilung,* a paramilitary wing of Adolf Hitler's Nazi Party. Wessel's political activities included participation in bloody street battles with Communists. A Communist gang eventually gunned him down.

History frequently pivots around small events. Wessel's demise is a case in point. His death would have been nearly inconsequential had he not written a poem some time before. Entitled "Raise High the Flag," it had been set in march time to a Viennese cabaret song from the turn of the century. As Wessel was dying, Joseph Goebbels, the mastermind behind Nazi propaganda, saw an opportunity.

Wessel's lyric immortalized those who had given their lives for the Nazi cause. Arranging to have the "Horst Wessel Song" sung at the conclusion of a Nazi meeting, Goebbels envisioned that it would become "the hymn of the German revolution." He was correct.

That same January a Jewish doctor, Sigmund Freud, went about his work in Vienna. Only a few weeks earlier he had finished a small book that would be among his most famous. In English it is called *Civilization and Its Discontents.* Among its final words are these: "Men have gained control over the forces of nature to such an extent that with their help they would have no difficulty in exterminating one another to the last man." Freud was also correct. Horst Wessel's song would help to prove the point.

As the Nazis sang that song in Berlin on a late February night in 1930, an infant destined to be even better known than Sigmund Freud was fast asleep. But the revolution glimpsed by Freud's premonition and rallied by Wessel's song would profoundly mark that Jewish girl, Anne Frank.

Years later, Anne Frank lived for months with her family in an Amsterdam hiding place. There she wrote the diary that is read annually by millions. Penned only days before the Franks were betrayed to the Nazis and only a few weeks before they were deported to Auschwitz, Anne Frank's best-known diary entry—it is dated July 15, 1944—contains the following testimony: "I see the world gradually being turned into a wilderness, I hear the ever approaching thunder, which will destroy us too." But in the same entry, Anne Frank also affirmed that "people are really good at heart," and she went on to say that her gloomy forecast would not be the last word. "If I look up into the heavens," she wrote, "I think that it will all come right, that this cruelty too will end, and that peace and tranquillity will return again."

Anne Frank was also correct, but how far is not yet clear. She was right about the gloomy part. As for the rest, perhaps the best one can say is that the jury is still out.

Horst Wessel, Sigmund Freud, and Anne Frank—those people never met. Yet they are linked together and to us in ways that must be fathomed if we are to take steps that can help us to live with our deepest differences, steps that might help us to move beyond hate.

Wessel's song honored the dead, but it moved men and women to hate and kill. If that song is silent now, there are too many to take its place. They form the counterpoint to Anne Frank's diary, which still moves its readers to bring out the good she saw in the human heart. *Civilization and Its Discontents,* the struggle between death and life, was Sigmund Freud's concern. His study works in between, trying to discern what makes people hate and love.

Freud could not be sure his research would have a happy outcome. Indeed the study of the Final Solution or "ethnic cleansing" or "sectarian violence" may produce despair or even show how to turn potential victims into corpses. But without comprehending what Horst Wessel's song can do, it is also unlikely that Anne Frank's diary can be read without a problematic sentimentality. Such sentimentality can obscure a more realistic and intense yearning that is needed to save children, women, and men from horrible truths, which shatter, in Anne Frank's phrase, "ideals, dreams, and cherished hopes."

Anne Frank lost her life at Bergen-Belsen. Human beings pledged to carry out the Final Solution killed her. That fact makes it all the more important to remember that her diary entry for July 15, 1944, contains this protesting affirmation: "I simply can't build up my hopes on a foundation consisting of confusion, misery, and death." By remembering Anne Frank, by studying not only her life and thought but also the hate-filled world that was their context, we may become better equipped to move "beyond the diary," to avoid sentimentality about it, and to make the informed, protesting affirmations that are so much needed within the difficulty of these times that are ours.

The Cult of Anne Frank: Returning to Basics

Henry R. Huttenbach

In the short span of twenty years, Anne Frank has been transformed and inflated into a legendary figure, a symbol of the Holocaust child-hero, a metaphor for the victims of genocide. Worse, the memory of Anne Frank has been packaged into traveling exhibits, along with promotional brochures. Furthermore, Anne's name is now bitterly fought over by rival organizations. At present, the Anne Frank House and Anne Frank Foundation are in court suing each other for the commercial rights to lease the name Anne Frank to souvenir manufacturers. Anne Frank has become a minor industry. Over 15 million copies of her diary have been sold. What has gone wrong?

What happened to the real Anne Frank? Who was she? What did she actually feel, say, and write? Who is responsible for the present sad state of affairs, which have included contentious court battles for the copyrights of her diary and the lucrative profits from its publication in over a dozen languages? Is this transformation of Anne into a larger-than-life enterprise what her father, Otto Frank, had intended when he became custodian of his daughter's manuscript after he emerged from the concentration camp? Most important, is this what she, Anne herself, had in mind while she faithfully composed her private daily thoughts? Is the present legacy of Anne Frank—the publicity, the hype, the exhibits, the rank commercialism, and the academic over-kill—what she wanted to convey to her readers?

In reply to these questions, it might be well to return to the basics and refresh our memories of the simple things, the human dimensions of Anne Frank and her words. Every now and then it becomes necessary to strip our accrued "knowledge" of people and their acts of the accumulated layers of "interpretations" that subsequent generations have superimposed and return to the original facts *before* they were transformed into myth, before Anne Frank became a cult figure of Holocaust studies, before scholars metamor-phosed her into a quasi saint, whose every word is revered as if it contained meanings well beyond the ken of the young author. Anne needs to be "liberated" from her hagi-ographers before further distortions of Anne Frank are in-flicted on her memory. It is incumbent on us to pay renewed attention to the absolute essentials of what we need to know about Anne to avoid falling for the tempta-tion of making distracting or superfluous interpretations.

In order to save Anne Frank from those determined to make an icon of her, we must remind ourselves of a handful of simple facts, whose very simplicity embody the real Anne and the tragedy of her life and death. All the rest is commentary. We must take care not to bury Anne under an avalanche of words not her own. If read sensitively, her diary entries are virtually self-explanatory; they call for a minimum of explanation and no exegesis. Her thoughts are not those of a mystic in need of explication. Her childlike eloquence makes crystal clear her inner and outer worlds. Anne the child-author should not be subordinated to the "insights" of an endless stream of analysts. On the contrary, we should approach Anne, open to *her* words, to *her* impressions, to *her* response to the frightful tragedy that enveloped her.

On reading Anne's diary one only needs to be informed of a few essentials: she and her family were Jewish refugees in Holland who had come from Germany in 1933, the year Hitler came to power and the Nazi Party started its vicious antisemitic campaign; in 1940, the year after World War II had broken out, Germany invaded Holland; by 1942, like thousands of other Jews, Anne and her family went into hiding to avoid deportation; the Franks and another family found refuge in an attic in a building in the middle of Amsterdam; and, for almost three years, Anne recorded her experiences, both as a fugitive refugee in danger of being discovered and sent to parts unknown and as a young maturing teenager.

In unadorned but often remarkably poetic language, Anne speaks of herself—of her dreams, of her encounters with young adulthood, and of her reconciliation with a life of stifling confinement. There are poignant signs of a budding author if allowed to develop her talents. But that was not to be. In May 1944, the Franks were discovered, arrested, and incarcerated. Anne did not survive; nor did her mother and sibling. Only her father, Otto Frank, returned in 1945, then to be given the manuscript of his murdered daughter's writings. Miraculously they had not been destroyed by the Germans. A friend of the family, Miep Gies, lovingly safeguarded the pages during the last months of the war.

In the diary, Anne invents a friend, Kitty, to whom she confides her innermost secrets about friends she misses, about school she cannot attend, and games she would like to play; about her fears of being caught, and about her hope for a happy future. She lived in a very small, cramped world, but she wrote about life beyond the walls of the attic. Interestingly, she barely mentions Jews and Judaism, largely because hers was a very typical, assimilated German Jewish family. She writes as an ordinary child-becoming-a-young-woman in cruelly unprecedented times.

More we do not need to know or say about Anne Frank. It is she who must speak and we who must listen. It is her words we must absorb, not ours about her. She is not a saint; she was no martyr; neither idol nor icon, neither symbol nor superheroine. She was "just" a child-victim of a merciless genocide aimed at Jews, one child of more than a million like her, lives snuffed out—murdered before their lives had even begun. If Anne has a face caught in a snapshot, so did the million other Jewish children whose photos were lost; her photograph should be seen alongside other snapshots, not alone, but together with the other children who also perished. They, too, had names. And we ought to recite their names, too, and not become fixated on the one child, on Anne alone. That does her memory discredit.

Her life was not made of the stuff of legends. Her life was so ordinary, so sadly typical, as were the fates of other Jewish children. They too lived in fear and hoped for hope against all hope; they too were arrested with their families, incarcerated, and exterminated. Anne is just *one* of them.

They were *all* Annes: young, ready for life, eager to live, but systematically destroyed. Her memory must not become a substitute for the other million.

Anne and her fellow Jewish children should not be reduced to abstract, academic thought, to metaphysical speculations, and pseudo-theological evaluations. That would be killing them once again by robbing them of the identity of what they once had been—children! Just children. To our good fortune one of them can speak to us across the decades and send us her memory of herself, she, the very, very young woman, robbed of her future. Out of respect to that memory, to the integrity of her words, one must avoid turning Anne Frank into a cultic figure serving the interests of others—whether academics, bureaucrats, or profiteers.

Part Three

Challenges

"Voices" of Anne Frank

Sidney Bolkosky

Some years ago, Joseph Berger, education editor of the *New York Times,* declared: "The question is not whether to continue reminding the world of the Holocaust, but how." More recently, as he received an Academy Award for *Schindler's List,* film director Steven Spielberg entreated educators to teach about the Holocaust. Hopeful as his plea may have sounded, it had the faint ring of facile Hollywood direction, not only failing to recognize the enormity of the request but, especially in light of the film, hinting at Hollywood-like, uplifting endings. How to teach about it without distortion, trivialization, or sentimentalization offers a major pedagogical challenge to any educator, but especially to secondary school teachers. Questions about *what, why,* or even *if* to teach about the Holocaust inextricably connect to *how* to teach about it; but the concern about method remains primary, both depending upon and determining the content.

There was no shortage of Holocaust materials in 1985 when my co-authors and I embarked on the *Life Unworthy of Life* project.[1] But virtually all of those materials were poorly conceived and/or painfully inadequate for teachers—often unhistorical, unsophisticated, and frightening to both teachers and students. Most curricula offered moralistic or shocking, sentimental or uninformed courses of study. They seemed either to have freed themselves artificially of the ghosts or to have been possessed by them. Some assumed missionary roles, and almost all seemed to presume prior knowledge on the part of the teachers. Of the more than 300 teaching tools listed in a synopsis of existing curricula in the United States, over half consisted of one or two lectures on atrocities. Still others hammered away with horrifyingly familiar films and pictures with little or no historical context or focus. American or European history textbooks also proved woefully inadequate, averaging one paragraph (approximately seventy words) on the Holocaust. In short, where the subject was taught, it was taught badly; more to the point, because of the poverty of resources, it was not being taught at all.

Most of those classes used one text, usually *The Diary of a Young Girl* by Anne Frank. The expurgated text of the diary contained little about Anne's personal conflicts, internal and external; very little of her insightful yet adolescent ruminations about her burgeoning sexuality; and even less reference to her Jewishness. In that text we hear the muted voice, near-romantic at times, of a hopeful victim, heroic to the last entry.

In 1996 South African producer-director-writer Jon Blair's film *Anne Frank Remembered* appeared to much critical acclaim. It later won an Academy Award for best documentary. Blair was no newcomer to the subject of the Holocaust, having produced the documentary *Schindler* in 1984. In that film, he made extensive and effective use of survivor testimonies, as well as of interviews with a variety of other people, including the mistress of Amon Goeth, the psychopathic killer and commandant of Plaszow. It became immediately clear at the outset of the film, which opens with a Spielberg-Schindler-like candle and plaintive Jewish music, that the film would not distort the reality of Anne's Jewishness. But more than images, voices set the tone, assume center stage, as it were. Blair explained that Barry Ackroyd, the brilliant cinematographer on *Anne Frank Remembered,* worked *from* voices of survivors and then tried to "ensure a rich visual texture which complements the interviews."[2] Indeed, the film broke new ground with its extensive use of survivor testimonies focusing not only on the likes of Miep Gies, the heroic woman who helped hide the Franks in Amsterdam for two years, but also on Jewish survivors who knew Anne and/or her family before and during the ordeal of the Holocaust. The interviews themselves differ from what most viewers have come to expect: they are not always pithy and moving 30- or 60-second sound bites. Many go on at length, the talk almost routine, distinctly not electrifying, but candid, honest, and setting a context for the rest of the story. We hear the voices of victims who survived—sometimes inarticulate, confused, tense, ambivalent, hesitant—but always honestly, with the subtext of loss audible and palpable. Those voices enhance the picture of Anne Frank and the historicity of the experience.

Holocaust writers have occasionally contrasted *The Diary of a Young Girl* with Elie Wiesel's *Night.*[3] The one ends, in a sense, where the other begins; and it is the latter that deals with the more familiar violence of the Holocaust. Now Blair has given us glimpses of what Anne's immersion into that violence was, at Auschwitz, on a death march, and, finally, in Bergen-Belsen. If we cannot conceive of Wiesel writing in his own memoir that he still believes people are good, can we now conceive that Anne Frank would have written that same sentence in Auschwitz? Blair's film strikes hard at the popular portrayal of this emblematic child, forces us to think differently about her and what she embodies. Clichés about the "triumph of the spirit" do not fit easily in this depiction and the denial or deemphasis of "the anxiety she lived with, the deprivations she suffered, and the gruesome outcome of her ordeal"[4] confront the viewer relentlessly throughout the production.

In part, the perceptions of Anne Frank began to change with the photographic exhibition "Anne Frank in the World: 1929–1945," produced by the Anne Frank Center and the Anne Frank Foundation. In that exhibit she is transformed from a symbol, an emblem—created by the diary and fostered by such productions as George Stevens's 1959 film—into a child, sharing qualities of most children. And, indeed, the exhibition may be interpreted as being about lost children—Anne and Margot Frank, Peter van Daan, and an estimated 1.5 million other Jewish children. The photographs reveal her in new ways, with friends, playing, mugging for the camera, bound to her sister, her father, and even to her mother. She emerges from those miraculously recovered photographs as part of a family, sometimes sentimental, usually smiling, eyes dark and wide; a child growing up in relative security and peace. We see Anne Frank in Amsterdam (not yet "in the world"), in her home, at the seaside, in the street with playmates. She materializes as a young girl, a child, real, concrete, and the more poignant for that. As with the diary, part of the power of the exhibit rests in our knowledge of the end, what will *not* be shown in the photographs or written in the book. Like Blair's film, the exhibit enhances, expands, and historicizes the diary.

Despite this realistic enlivening of the story, the catalogue of the exhibit harkens back to a naive and sentimental form. The preface opens with the question: "Had Anne Frank, a typical child, lived next door, could she have counted on us for help during the Nazi regime?"[5] That query resonates with earlier approaches to the story of Anne Frank and seems too simplistic and disingenuous to offer to students. Such questions of rescue are not what breathe through the photographs, the diary, and the history of the Holocaust. In that sad and painful history, educators might hope to convey children's fear and the ubiquitous sense of anguish. That will constitute a deeper appreciation of what the Holocaust means, not questions that seem almost prayerful, reassuring, reducing the complexities of the epoch to simplistic dilemmas.

With *Anne Frank Remembered,* we gain glimpses of the previously unseen. Twenty days before the Germans shipped those hidden in the Secret Annex to the transit camp at Westerbork and then to Auschwitz, Anne wrote:

> It's utterly impossible for me to build my life on a foundation of chaos, suffering and death. I see the world being slowly transformed into a wilderness, I hear the approaching thunder that, one day, will destroy us too, I feel the suffering of millions. And yet, when I look up at the sky, I somehow feel that everything will change for the better, that this cruelty too shall end, that peace and tranquillity will return once more.[6]

Like the more famous passage, "in spite of everything," that ends with her conviction of goodness triumphant, this passage reverberates with hope and redemption. Could she have written or spoken those words in Auschwitz or Bergen-Belsen? Survivors who recalled her in those awful places, some in Blair's film, described a child near madness with hunger and disease, sunken-eyed and weeping.

We cannot know how she would have thought or felt after the boxcar, the arrival, selection, and subsequent humiliation of the Auschwitz experience. But survivors who speak of those ordeals do not, as a rule, voice visions of redemptive peace and tranquillity. Nor do they describe themselves as clinging to hope for humankind in the heart of darkness. They speak reticently, in a language that they know remains inadequate to communicate the reality of the Holocaust: "Auschwitz—what is that? How can I explain it to you," breathed one woman.[7] The word, the name, carried such density for her, so many associations that have no apposite experiential context for listeners from the rest of the world, that she frustratedly wept over that inability. "Why should I bother," exclaimed another, his voice tinged with contempt, "you won't understand it anyway—it's my experience, not yours. You weren't there."[8] From this paradox of frustration coupled with a frequent compulsion to tell, few if any survivors speak of an end to that cruelty so that "peace and tranquillity will return again." Survivor testimonies, in short, like Wiesel's *Night,* or other memoirs, do not leave listeners or readers feeling better. Unlike popular media presentations, such testimony does not reassure or buoy us. We are left with sadness—profound, empty, and problematic in terms of educational goals.

In addressing this puzzle, Primo Levi began to despair over the tendency to simplify the Holocaust, lamenting the terrible simplifiers.[9] Early forms of *The Diary of Anne Frank* and its uses in classrooms epitomize that tendency. It is a trend continued and intensified by the popular acceptance of media productions like *Schindler's List,* which, their excellent aesthetic merits aside, invite positive and warmly hopeful feelings about the Holocaust. They present heroic rescuers—Miep Gies, Oskar Schindler—matched by angelic and forgiving victims like Anne Frank and provide a redemptive lesson derived from the worst of historical epochs. But, as Levi knew, and, perhaps, as Anne Frank knew in Bergen-Belsen, nothing good or redemptive came from the Holocaust—nothing.

At the end of Jon Blair's film, one of Anne's friends, a survivor of Auschwitz and Bergen-Belsen, stands again at the last place she saw her friend. A cold, barren field behind her, dwarfed by the barbed wire that had once separated the two girls, where Anne had wept before her, she reflects upon their fates. Ironic, she notes, that Anne, known for her hope, did not survive. "And here I am [pause] I don't know." A fitting conclusion, although Blair decides to return to the only filmed image of Anne Frank. A year before she went into the Secret Annex, she leaned from a window and happily watched newlyweds as they left the building. Stunned audiences now have seen her: smiling, briefly glimpsed, the child on the brink of destruction. And now that picture draws our attention to the life she might have had—marriage, children, career. How painful to regard, knowing she was soon to be cut down with her family and some 115,000 Dutch Jews who "in a murderous present ... became the victims of their peaceful past."[10]

Notes

1. Sidney Bolkosky, Betty Rotberg Elias, and David Harris, *Life Unworthy of Life: A Holocaust Curriculum* (New York/Chicago: Glencoe Press, 1986).

2. Jon Blair, *Anne Frank Remembered* (Sony Pictures Classics, 1996).

3. See, for example, Alvin Rosenfeld, "The Anne Frank We Remember," *Dimensions* 5 (1989): 9–13.

4. Ibid.

5. Joke Kniesmeyer, *Anne Frank in the World, 1929–1945* (Amsterdam: Anne Frank Stichtung, 1985).

6. *Anne Frank: The Diary of a Young Girl: The Definitive Edition,* ed. Otto H. Frank and Mirjam Pressler; trans. Susan Massotty (New York: Doubleday, 1995), 332.

7. Cyla W., "Voice/Vision" Holocaust Survivor Oral History Archive, University of Michigan–Dearborn.

8. Alex E., ibid.

9. Primo Levi, *The Drowned and the Saved* (New York: Simon and Schuster, 1988), 20.

10. Louis de Jong, *The Destruction of Dutch Jewry* (London: Harvard University Press, 1990).

Toward a Proper Legacy

G. Jan Colijn

There is little question that *The Diary of Anne Frank* retains a powerful, evocative role as the main gateway to the Holocaust for many people, especially youngsters, but one must be dismayed with the way the diary has sometimes been used to create an image of the Netherlands during World War II and the Holocaust that is at considerable odds with reality. That popular image, of the good Dutch, is still not fully extinct, although scholars know better. There are some, Judith Miller and Sylvain Ephimenco, for instance, who argue that the Dutch managed a very large post–World War II public relations operation by using the diary—and this is the central point—to pretend that all Jews were in hiding and that the entire Dutch population was in resistance.[1]

In this context, readers must know that today's Dutch—I am Dutch myself—tend to be rather self-possessed about their progressiveness, quick to indict racism across their borders, while belittling it at home. The reader can imagine what a hit Daniel Goldhagen's book, *Hitler's Willing Executioners: Ordinary Germans and the Holocaust* (New York: Knopf, 1996) was last year, fixing the blame for the Holocaust, as it does, firmly and exclusively on the "other" side of the Dutch-German border. However, the old Dutch self-image can no longer coexist with a full facing up to our failings in the war, to a full and national recognition that millions of Dutch bystanders—without much moral leadership from the elites—allowed nearly their entire Jewish population to be deported. The first issue, then, is not that we do not know the bitter facts of that horrendous reality, but that Anne Frank's diary has sometimes been used to feed the myth of the "heroic" Dutch who resisted the Nazis, among other things, by hiding Jews.[2] Therefore, the demythologization of the "good" Dutch is at the center of an honest reshaping of Dutch history.

Specific aspects of such historiography, as for example, the complicity of Dutch authorities, the complacency of the Dutch government-in-exile in London, and the silence of Radio Oranje—the broadcast tool of the government-in-exile—need to be further explored and highlighted. One example of such an exploration has just been published by Nanda van der Zee, *Om erger te voorkamen* (Amsterdam: Meulenhoff, 1997). Van der Zee comes to harsh conclusions. The Dutch elites were, at best, indifferent to the fate of the Jews, and their failure to set a moral example and to be Cassandras contributed, in van der Zee's view, to the disproportionate destruction of Dutch Jews. Unlike Goldhagen's thesis, the issue in the Netherlands is not the virulent antisemitism of the public at large, but the abdication of moral responsibility by many at the top of Dutch society. Conversely, the record of the resistance and its courageous illegal press is generally well known. There is, for example, ample and compelling need to emphasize the role of those righteous gentiles such as the extraordinary Miep Gies, who helped the people hiding in the Secret Annex, or that truly heroic Marion Pritchard who is featured in the documentary film and book *The Courage to Care: Rescuers of Jews during the Holocaust* (New York: New York University Press, 1986).

A critical goal of education should be to show that righteous behavior *was* possible in Holland, even under the most difficult of circumstances. It is, however, also worth exploring whether there is a relationship between the small but hard-core Nazi support in the Netherlands prior to World War II and the fact that one-third of the Jews in hiding were betrayed, a point alluded to in the "Anne Frank in the World" exhibition. In short, the record of the righteous must be balanced against *other* harsh realities: we must balance these various views if we want to reflect on Anne Frank's diary in a meaningful way. The first task, then, is to demythologize the image of the "good" Dutch in World War II, especially abroad where, beyond Holocaust scholars, far less of the ongoing debate on Dutch war history will reach an audience. One should read Jacob Presser's *The Destruction of the Dutch Jews* (New York: Dutton, 1969) in conjunction with *The Diary of Anne Frank*; and, once it is translated, van der Zee's latest treatise.

The second task is to make responsible linkages between Anne's story and events today. Of course, Anne's legacy and her voice, as it comes to us through the diary, stand as a warning to all those concerned with discrimination on the basis of color, culture, or creed. It was inspiring enough to have been of comfort to Nelson Mandela when he was imprisoned. But let us not dehistoricize the story in order to make rushed connections to Rwanda, to Cambodia, or to Bosnia. The media are only too ready to draw superficial parallels between the Holocaust and today's atrocities. The Bosnian crisis, for example, is uncritically compared with the Holocaust, ignoring the fact that the former is a civil war—a critical difference with the Holocaust. There is a tendency to make uncritical comparisons between the Holocaust and other atrocities. Those invariably unanalytical comparisons are problematic in two ways: first, the presumed atrocities committed by nations other than Germany are used to normalize the Holocaust to a level of unacceptable ordinariness; second, nations who did commit such atrocities in their history belittle such realities by arguing, "At least it was not as bad as the destruction of the Jews," or "At least we are not as bad as the Germans." We like to leave evil in Germany, as I have argued elsewhere.[3]

When we dehistoricize the story, we also often "de-judaize" the story, which is the third issue. One of the many wonderful qualities of Jon Blair's Oscar-winning documentary, *Anne Frank Remembered,* is that it does not "de-judaize" the story. Blair highlights the German-Jewish origins not only of the Franks but also of their neighbors and friends, such as Hannah Goslar, "Lies" in the diary, arguably Anne's best friend. The film notes Hitler's victory at the ballot box, depicts vitriolic antisemitic propaganda in the film *The Eternal Jew,* shows Dutch Nazi sympathizers, and the Nazi infiltration of the Dutch police service, including even in Prime Minister Colijn's cabinet office. The film is particularly effective in depicting the gradual, never-ending series of anti-Jewish decrees issued early in the Nazi occupation: by 1942 no area of Jewish life was beyond German control. Hitler's war was a war against what the Nazis called "judeo-bolshevism." What the Germans did in the

Netherlands was to wage war against the Jews. The destruction of Dutch Jewry was made possible by ever-tightening isolation from non-Jews. And whereas the cultivated and prosperous Franks had considerable means to facilitate the move to the Secret Annex, their exceptional position renders their eventual unexceptional fate even more poignant. At the core of Anne Frank's story is the fact that she is a Jew, and we betray her memory if we downplay the very reason she died.

A fourth task to remember is not to turn Anne Frank into an icon or a saint. Jon Blair's film normalizes Anne as a child by concentrating on her childhood before the hiding period, and before the last seven months. There is the wonderful recollection of Hanneli Goslar—now known by her late husband's name, as Hannah Pick—who recalls that her mother used to say: "God knows everything but Anne knows everything better." Another of Anne's contemporaries remembers her as a "naughty" and "impertinent" child. We are not interested, of course, in some antiseptic deconstruction. Anne was a precocious child, talented, quirky, but normal, not a saint. What we must rail against is the so-called cheap sentimentality, as Hannah Arendt put it in *Eichmann in Jerusalem*.[4] It is distasteful to think of Anne Frank in terms so elevated that her image approaches the vulgar idolization surrounding someone like Evita Peron.

The screen and stage adaptations of the diary not only dehistoricize and "de-judaize," they also are full of a misplaced emphasis on naiveté, optimism, and attempts to use the diary as a metaphor for universalist suffering. I understand that when schools want to put on a play, it is natural to use the diary because it resonates so deeply with youngsters as they begin to learn the relationship of self with others. But I do not like using it to teach kids how to act. It is too sacred for that. Jon Blair told me that a few years ago the play was put on somewhere in California and the actress playing Anne was so bad that when the Germans showed up to arrest the family, the audience shouted, "She is in the attic, she is in the attic."[5] Apocryphal? Probably, but a good vignette about the point that needs to be made: think carefully about the purpose for which the diary is read or staged.

A word on misplaced optimism, the fifth issue. We must not give Anne's story and legacy the wrong spin. There is probably no line in the diary more misused than "in spite of everything, I still believe people are good at heart." Alvin Rosenfeld, for example, has noted that misuse. He writes that the "projection of single images of ubiquitous and compelling power" can create false popular perceptions.[6] When Hannah Pick visited us at Stockton College in October 1996, a student asked the following question: "If Anne Frank had survived, would Anne *still* believe people were good at heart?" Anne's best friend shook her head ruefully, and softly said no.

The problem, as Judith Doneson has pointed out, is that Anne's optimism too often is used to rehabilitate Christianity. The issue, of course, goes well beyond the shortcomings of the Dutch people in their abandonment of the Jews during the war. Anne becomes a martyr, not a victim, someone to inspire us, not someone to be mourned. She is not a "secular saint" who should bear the suffering for the viewer or the reader. By emphasizing Anne's optimism and not her much darker writing, we turn her phrases into a kind of universal forgiveness for the failure of Christianity during the Holocaust: only the victims have the right to do that, not us.[7]

My sixth issue centers around Miep Gies and the other helpers. Often, they become the central theme. They are heroes, of course, but again, Christians should not seek redemption behind Miep's skirts. In the 1959 movie *The Diary of Anne Frank*, we know from the opening shots, as Judith Doneson, Jacqueline Berke, and others have noted, that the "good" Christian Miep saved the diary and because of her, Anne's legacy lives on. "Virtually the first shot in the film is of a church. In the soundtrack church bells ring throughout."[8] It is comforting to us to see "good" Christians at work. But the very fact of the matter is that the Holocaust happened in the very center of Christianity and Western civilization. In that context, most scholars (e.g., Berke, Doneson, Rosenfeld) agree that the film is a grievous misconstruction. Redemption, hope, and forgiveness simply should not be the central themes in teaching about *The Diary of Anne Frank*. The corollary problem with the stage and screen versions of the diary is that they affirm the theme of the Jew as passive, as weak, as a loser, or, to put it in today's vernacular, as a wimp in need of protection. The other side of this coin is that the Christians are heroes (rescuers!). Even when villains, Christians are at least active rather than passive. This active-passive (Christian-Jewish) dichotomy is so stubborn that one may conclude, as Susan Kray does, that it has become "part of the Holocaust genre."[9]

As of this writing, the news has reached me that those who control the rights to the play have now consented to have the text altered to reflect some of the criticisms, and to reflect on what we know now that the playwrights did not know when they wrote it years ago. This, of course, is excellent news. It means that the possibility now exists to right some of shortcomings of the play and to bring it perhaps more closely in line with the diary itself but also with other sources we now have, for example, the memoirs of Miep Gies.

With the beginning of mandated Holocaust education in several states, Anne's diary will continue to be the main window on the Holocaust for many students. It may be the only full-length book students read about the Holocaust. If we are to have respect for Anne *and* for a reasonably balanced portrayal of what happened in Holland during World War II and the Holocaust, students should read Presser's book, or Marga Minco's *Bitter Herbs: A Little Chronicle* (New York: Penguin, 1991), or watch Willy Lindwer's documentary film, *The Last Seven Months of Anne Frank.* While it is not explicitly about Anne Frank, one can learn about what Dutch women went through in the camps. Another good book to read is Werner Warmbrunn, *The Dutch Under German Occupation, 1940–1945* (San Francisco: Stanford University Press, 1963). The Anne Frank story deserves a context, and these books and this film, read and viewed in conjunction with her diary, can provide it.

Finally, as educators, we should set some specific educational goals when teaching about *The Diary of Anne Frank.* Let us take our lead from the new exhibit, "Anne Frank: A History for Today," which opened in Vienna in October 1996. The goals of that exhibition are instructive:

- to inform about the history of the Holocaust;
- to show that in each society there are differences be-

tween people (cultural, ethnic, and religious.) Every effort to (re)organize a society on the basis of "racial purity," religion, or ethnic groups leads to purges. Minorities that do not fit the idea are discriminated against, set apart, persecuted, and sometimes murdered;
- to make students think about concepts such as tolerance, mutual respect, human rights, and democracy;
- to show that a society in which diversity is respected does not come about by itself.

Such goals, it seems to me, are exactly the right ones. In setting goals such as these, we help the diary to live on but not in a vacuum, not in cheap sentimentality, mythology, misuse, or in the flaccid universalism that surrounds comparison between the Holocaust and other atrocities. We need to treat Anne Frank's story responsibly. She deserves no less than that.

Notes

1. Sylvain Ephimenco, *Hollandse kost* (Amsterdam: Contact, 1994), 89–95; Judith Miller, *One by One by One: Facing the Holocaust* (New York: Simon and Schuster, 1990), 93–111.
2. Nanda van der Zee, "The Recurrent Myth of Dutch Heroism in the Second World War and Anne Frank as a Symbol," in *The Netherlands and Nazi Genocide: Papers of the 21st Annual Scholars' Conference*, ed. G. Jan Colijn and Marcia S. Littell (Lewiston, NY: Edwin Mellon Press, 1992), 1–14.
3. See Didier Pollefeyt and G. Jan Colijn, "Leaving Evil in Germany: The Questionable Success of Goldhagen in the Low Countries," in *Hyping the Holocaust—Scholars Answer Goldhagen*, ed. Franklin H. Littell (East Rockaway, NY: Cummings and Hathaway, 1997), 1–18.
4. Hannah Arendt, *Eichmann in Jerusalem* (New York: Viking, 1965).

5. See Jacqueline Berke, "The Diary of Anne Frank: Widely Acclaimed but Wantonly Betrayed," paper delivered at the Remembering for the Future II conference, Berlin, Germany, March 1994. For an excellent review on wrong-headed popularization, see Alvin H. Rosenfeld, "Popularization and Memory: The Case of Anne Frank," in *Lessons and Legacies,* ed. Peter Hayes (Evanston, IL: Northwestern University Press, 1991), 243–278.

6. See Rosenfeld, "Popularization and Memory," 243.

7. See Judith Doneson, "Feminine Stereotypes of Jews in Holocaust Films: Focus on the Diary of Anne Frank," in Colijn and Littell, eds., *The Netherlands and the Nazi Genocide,* 139–153, 150. The martyr-victim analogy is Alvin H. Rosenfeld's. See "The Anne Frank We Remember," *Dimensions* 5 (1989): 9–13; the rehabilitation theme can also be found in Berke, "The Diary of Anne Frank."

8. Berke, "The Diary of Anne Frank."

9. See, for example, the critique of Ilene Rosenzweig, "Watching Schindler," *Forward* 10 (December 1993), as cited in Susan Kray, "What Have the Christian Churches Failed to Confront? Communication, Ethics and Religious Institutions," in *The Holocaust—Lessons for the Third Generation—Studies in the Shoah,* ed. Dominick A. Iorio et al. (Lanham, MD: University Press of America, 1997), 149–165, 157. The quote is on the same page.

Anne Frank in the World: A Study Guide

Mary Johnson and Carol Rittner

For more than a decade, people all across the United States, as well as in several foreign countries, have had the opportunity to view a photographic exhibition entitled "Anne Frank in the World: 1929–1945." Using hundreds of photographs with text, the exhibition provides a profile of the rise of a totalitarian society—Nazi Germany—in which racism and discrimination determined governmental policies in domestic and foreign affairs. In addition to documenting the lives of the Frank family (beginning with Anne's birth in Germany in 1929 and the family's move to Amsterdam in 1933, soon after Adolf Hitler was appointed chancellor of Germany), the exhibition draws attention to the resurgence of bigotry and racism in many parts of the world, especially in Europe and North America. Among other things, the exhibition is intended to provoke viewers into thinking about the choices they are making today, living in the final years of the twentieth century. Whenever it is in a particular city, teachers and clergy from area schools, churches, and synagogues bring students to it, often reading and studying Anne Frank's *The Diary of Young Girl* in conjunction with the exhibition.

The purpose of this study guide is to give educators a practical resource they can use to prepare students for the "Anne Frank in the World" exhibit, to generate student discussion about Anne Frank and her diary, and to encourage discussion about the ever-present dangers in society of racism, discrimination, and the rise of totalitarianism. The guide is divided into six themes:

- Who Is Anne Frank?
- Society and the Individual;
- Discrimination Is Cruel and Irrational;
- Ordinary People Discriminate;
- Discrimination Is a Matter of Personal Choice;
- Discrimination Continues Today.

These themes are intended to help students to reflect on the choices and decisions individuals, groups, and nations made during the Nazi era in Germany and occupied Europe (1933–1945) and to encourage them to think about how they make decisions in their own lives today. Specific references in the questions are made to the definitive edition of the diary that appeared in 1995 (Doubleday). This edition contains passages that had been omitted from the original 1947 edition.

Who Is Anne Frank?

"Anne Frank in the World" provides background information about Anne, her family, their life in Germany and Holland before World War II and the Holocaust, and about the ordeal the Franks and their friends in the Secret Annex faced while they were in hiding. The exhibition introduces the concept of rescue through the employees and friends of Mr. Frank who helped him and his family before their subsequent betrayal, arrest, and deportation to Westerbork, Auschwitz, and Bergen-Belsen. Viewers also learn about Anne's precious diary, which she named "Kitty," a close friend with whom she could share her innermost thoughts and feelings. During her twenty-eight months in hiding, Anne regularly turned to Kitty to reflect on events inside and outside the Secret Annex. In the diary, the reader learns about a young teenager coming of age as she struggles to define herself as an independent person, albeit one caught in the traumatic and tragic circumstances of her time. Many of Anne's questions are pertinent to adolescents of every era:

> How can I be free of my parents, relatives, and teachers telling me what to do and who I am? How can I get others to take me seriously? How do I deal with peer pressure? When is it necessary to obey laws and rules incompatible with my own values? What are my values? How can I deal with my feelings of loneliness?

The final entry in the diary is dated August 1, 1944, three days before the Gestapo and the German occupation police broke into the Secret Annex and arrested the inhabitants. Still in the process of discovering her own identity, Anne feels misunderstood by an adult world that seems to scrutinize her every move and word, but we learn no more of Anne's inner dialogue because all the inhabitants of the Secret Annex are deported to the Nazi death camps. Kitty is left scattered on the floor in the secret hiding place.

Sometime later, two of the people who had been helping

Anne and the others, pick up the scattered pages of the diary. After the war, Miep Gies gives the precious pages to Anne's father, Otto Frank, the sole survivor of the Secret Annex. Before allowing Anne's diary to be published in 1947, Mr. Frank carefully edited sections of it he considered unsuitable (for example, all the unfavorable comments about Mrs. Frank as well as the various references Anne made to her awakening sexuality).

Society and the Individual

At the heart of the exhibit is the story of the Frank family and the impact world events had on their lives as they lived successively in Frankfurt, in Amsterdam, in the transit camp of Westerbork, and in the Nazi death camps in Poland and Germany. The Franks were persecuted because they were Jews, not because of anything they had done or failed to do. As the exhibition points out, choices for Jewish and non-Jewish victims of the Nazis became increasingly restricted during the Third Reich, and, after 1941, choices for Jews literally became nonexistent. The viewer sees photographs of such people as Anton Mussert, leader of the Dutch Nazi Party, and Baldur von Schirach, head of the Hitler Youth, both of whom made deliberate choices to sustain the Nazi program. There are photographs of Hans and Sophie Scholl. The Sholls, who were initially drawn to the Hitler Youth and the leadership of Hitler, deliberately chose to reject National Socialism when they realized how restrictive and destructive the movement was. As university students, they openly opposed the Nazis and organized a protest among other students and some faculty. They were caught and hanged for their defiance, but their stand gave strength to others to carry on resistance activities.

Because the individual choices of individual people are central to the "Anne Frank in the World" exhibition, teachers might draw attention to questions such as the following.

Questions

What factors influence how we make choices? What factors influence how we think about others? How do we know who we are, given the media messages that bombard us day after day? What are the pressures from family, school, and church that continually have an impact on us? How does peer pressure affect our identity? Our decision-making process? Our choices? Throughout the diary Anne reminds us that her perceptions as a young woman influence how she sees the world and thinks of herself and others. To what extent do you believe that gender influences the decision-making process?

Discrimination Is Cruel and Irrational

Anne's growing-up experience took place within the context of Nazi Germany's invasion and occupation of Holland. Throughout her diary, Anne makes reference to events taking place in Holland and across Europe and how those events had their impact on their lives in hiding. The exhibition draws attention to events that decisively affected the Franks and thousands of other Dutch Jews. To understand how they became victims of discrimination during the Third Reich, one should review the rise of Nazism in Germany and its spread throughout Europe in the late 1930s and during World War II. Among the questions one could discuss with students are the following.

Questions

How did the Nazis carry out the ideas originally set forth in Hitler's *Mein Kampf?* Why did the great majority of Germans not recognize the small steps that were whittling away their human rights? Why did neighbor turn against neighbor during the Nazi era? What role did terror play in helping the Nazis consolidate their power and authority? (Select specific references in the diary in which Anne indicates how the Nazi use of terror is turning neighbors against one another.) Which photographs in the exhibition sharply remind the viewer that the Nazi use of terror was part of everyday existence in German-occupied Europe? At what point was it too late to prevent the Nazis from gaining power? How did the Nazis use the media to mold public opinion?

On January 20, 1942, leading civilian and military officials of the Third Reich met at Wannsee, a villa on the outskirts of Berlin, to plan the "final solution of the Jewish problem." They discussed the developing plan to murder the Jews of Europe. According to this plan, under the pretext that they would be given work and adequate food, trains were to transport Jews to special areas of concentration and then to death camps located in Eastern Europe. The major death camps—Chelmno, Auschwitz, Belzec,

Sobibor, Treblinka, and Majdanek—were located in strategic areas of German-occupied Poland, close to major rail lines. Jews in the Warsaw ghetto were sent to Treblinka, and Jews in the ghettos of Lublin and Lvov were sent to Belzec. Auschwitz, the largest death camp, received Jews from all over Europe. People in areas surrounding the camps did little to intervene. Relatively speaking, only a small minority of individuals helped Jews during the Holocaust. The overwhelming majority of Jewish children—scholars estimate between a million and a million and a half died—including Anne and Margot Frank, perished during the Holocaust. Only about 150,000 Jewish children survived.

Questions

Using selections from Anne Frank's diary, trace the implementation of antisemitic legislation in Holland. Why were Anne and other Jews in her community surprised by the introduction of antisemitic measures in Holland? Given the increasing restrictions on Jews living in Holland that Anne enumerates in her entry of June 15, 1942, why didn't the Franks and other Jews emigrate? As a teenager, have you ever experienced discrimination from peers? From adults? Have you ever seen classmates, or other people, humiliated for being different? What were your reactions to such treatment? What examples can you find in the news that suggest that some young people today are being educated "for hatred"? What can be done to counter such education? What analogies do you find between "ethnic cleansing" in former Yugoslavia and the Nazi policy for making Europe *judenrein* (Jew-free)? How are they similar and different?

Ordinary People Discriminate

Nazi propaganda played a key role in turning neighbor against neighbor in the Third Reich. It stereotyped the "enemies" of the community and identified these "enemies" with the economic, social, and political difficulties confronting the nation. Nazi propaganda, for example, portrayed Jews as parasites and offered a "scientific" explanation that Jews were in an arrested state of human development. Nazi literature and art represented Jews as "bugs" or "vermin" that had to be exterminated so that society could flourish.

The exhibition shows the special interest Nazis took in indoctrinating youth with their ideology in every aspect of their lives, as, for example, in areas such as the family, the school, and extracurricular activities. Textbooks in all subjects, including mathematics, stressed the superiority of the so-called Aryan race. A common subject in German schools was "race science" in which students practiced measuring the heads of each other in order to determine an individual's racial characteristics. Questions such as the following could be discussed.

Questions

What is discrimination? Propaganda? Indoctrination? Can you give any examples of these practices today? How did Nazi propaganda contribute to the process of making Jews seem like "the other"? What forms of media did the Nazis use for their propaganda? Can you think of groups in your own city, county, state, country that are depicted as "the other"? What can be done about this "ordinary" practice carried out by "ordinary people"? How do average, even admirable people become dehumanized by the circumstances impacting on them? What is the effect of school curricula and popular culture (art, music, sports, magazines, the Internet) on thinking, attitudes, and development of young people? Of people of whatever age?

Discrimination Is a Matter of Personal Choice

"Anne Frank in the World" illustrates the diversity of responses people made who were not targeted by the Nazis as "enemies of the State" or as *untermenshen* (subhumans) during the Third Reich. Those who were not victims of the Nazis and their collaborators had a *choice* as to whether or not they would discriminate against those who were victims. Anne discusses these people and groups in her diary. By 1941, when the Nazis began in earnest to implement the "final solution of the Jewish problem," Jews were left with what has become known as a "choiceless choice." They had no viable moral options for survival in the "topsy-turvy" world Anne describes in her diary. Teachers could focus on questions such as the following.

Questions

On May 8, 1944, Anne writes that "the world's been turned upside down." Traditional morality no longer characterizes relations: decent people are punished while "the lowest of the low" prevail. How did Anne keep abreast of the topsy-turvy world while she was hidden in the Annex? Who is part of your universe of moral concern? Can you imagine a situation in which you would risk your life to save the life of a family member? A friend? A stranger? Have you ever turned your back on, or pretended you did not notice, a person who was being discriminated against? Made fun of? Harmed? What is the difference between a bystander, a perpetrator, and a helper? What makes the difference in the role one plays in life? What does the term "desk murderer" mean? What is meant by critical judgment? Conformity? Obedience? Dissent? What enables a person to choose life, rather than death? What enables a person to be *for* human beings, rather than *against* human beings? For dignity, rather than for discrimination? What helps, or hinders, people of any age from knowing the difference between right and wrong?

Discrimination Continues Today

"Anne Frank in the World" ends by challenging viewers to think about the closing years of the twentieth century. There are photographs of skinheads and neo-Nazis, racial assaults, and antisemitic graffiti, "ethnic cleansing," and other forms of violence and human rights abuses. Questions such as the following could be raised.

Questions

What are ways today to prevent the abuse of human rights and the utter disregard for human life such as occurred in the 1930s and 1940s? What can we do in our schools, churches, synagogues, and neighborhoods to promote caring, tolerance, and respect for one another? What policies can governments support that will encourage citizens to live with their deepest differences, political, social, economic, and religious? Describe an incident of hatred and violence that has taken place recently in your school or community? Who were the perpetrators? Victims? Bystanders? Helpers? What were the causes of the hatred and violence? What motivates those who try to ameliorate prejudice, discrimination, and violence?

An interesting exercise is to ask students to reflect on a comment attributed to the German Lutheran pastor Martin Niemoeller, a man who in the early 1930s supported Hitler and the Nazis, but later opposed them. As a result, he was arrested and sent to Dachau concentration camp. After his liberation by the American army, he reportedly said,

> In Germany, when the Nazis came for the communists, I didn't speak up because I wasn't a communist. Then they came for the trade unionists, but I said nothing because I wasn't a trade unionist. Then they came for the Catholics, and I kept quiet because I wasn't a Catholic. Later they came for the Jews, but I wasn't a Jew so I didn't say a word. Then, they came for me, and by that time there was no one left to speak up for me.

In conclusion, the following questions might be raised.

Questions

The diary and play about Anne Frank are read and reread yearly throughout the world by young people. Why do you think that Anne's writing continues to interest them decades after Anne was murdered in the Bergen-Belsen concentration camp? What do you consider her most important message?

The "Anne Frank in the World" exhibition is a teachable moment, an opportunity to think about what happened in Nazi Germany and occupied Europe during the 1930s and 1940s, years when the bonds of human obligation did not hold. It gives teachers and students alike the chance to study the past in order to raise questions about what can happen, as well as what is happening, in the world today.

Selected Bibliography, Videography, and Teaching Resources

Selected Bibliography

Anne Frank's Tales from the Secret Annex, trans. Ralph Manheim and Michel Mok. New York: Washington Square Press, 1983.

Anne Frank: The Diary of a Young Girl, trans. B.M. Mooyaart. New York: Doubleday, 1967.

Barnouw, David, and Gerrold van der Stroom, eds. *The Diary of Anne Frank: The Critical Edition,* trans. Arnold J. Pomerans and B.M. Mooyart. New York: Doubleday, 1989.

Bauer, Yehuda, and Nili Keren. *A History of the Holocaust,* New York: Franklin Watts, 1982.

Berenbaum, Michael, ed. *A Mosaic of Victims: Non-Jews Persecuted and Murdered by the Nazis.* New York: New York University Press, 1990.

Block, Gay, and Malka Drucker. *Rescuers: Portraits of Moral Courage in the Holocaust.* New York: Holmes & Meier, 1992.

Boas, Jacob. *Boulevard des Miseres: The Story of Transit Camp Westerbork.* Hamden, CT: Archon Books, 1985.

Brenner, Rachael F. *Writing as Resistance: Four Women Confronting the Holocaust, Edith Stein, Simone Weil, Anne Frank, and Etty Hillesum.* State College: Pennsylvania State University, 1997.

Colijn, G. Jan, and Marcia S. Littell, eds. *The Netherlands and Nazi Genocide.* Lewiston, NY: Edwin Mellon Press, 1992.

de Jong, Louis. *The Destruction of Dutch Jewry.* London: Harvard University Press, 1990.

Eman, Diet, and James Schaap. *Things We Couldn't Say.* Grand Rapids, MI: W.B. Eerdmans, 1994.

117

Fogelman, Eva. *Conscience and Courage: Rescuers of Jews during the Holocaust.* New York: Anchor Books, 1994.

Frank, Otto, and Mirjam Pressler, eds. *Anne Frank: The Diary of a Young Girl: The Definitive Edition.* Trans. Susan Masotty. New York: Doubleday, 1995.

Gies, Miep, and Alison Leslie Gold. *Anne Frank Remembered: The Story of the Woman Who Helped to Hide the Frank Family.* New York: Simon and Schuster, 1988.

Gushee, David P. *The Righteous Gentiles of the Holocaust: A Christian Interpretation.* Minneapolis: Fortress Press, 1994.

Hayes, Peter, ed. *Lessons and Legacies: The Meaning of the Holocaust in a Changing World.* Evanston, IL: Northwestern University Press, 1991.

Hillesum, Etty. *An Interrupted Life,* trans. Arnold Pomerans. New York: Washington Square Press, 1985.

Hurwitz, Johanna. *Anne Frank: Life in Hiding.* New York: Jewish Publication Society, 1988.

Kniesmeyer, Joke. *Anne Frank in the World, 1929–1945.* Amsterdam: Anne Frank Stichtung, 1985.

Lindwer, Willy. *The Last Seven Months of Anne Frank,* trans. Alison Meersschaert. New York: Pantheon Books, 1991.

Miller, Judith. *One by One by One: Facing the Holocaust.* New York: Simon and Schuster, 1990.

Presser, Jacob. *The Destruction of the Dutch Jews,* trans. Arnold Pomerans. New York: Dutton, 1969.

Rittner, Carol, and Sondra Meyers, eds. *The Courage to Care: Rescuers of Jews During the Holocaust.* New York: New York University Press, 1986.

Rittner, Carol, and John K. Roth., eds. *Different Voices: Women and the Holocaust.* New York: Paragon House, 1993.

Rubenstein, Richard L., and John K. Roth. *Approaches to Auschwitz: The Holocaust and its Legacy.* Atlanta: John Knox Press, 1987.

Schloss, Eva, and Evelyn J. Kent. *Eva's Story: A Survivor's Tale by the Step-Sister of Anne Frank.* London: W.H. Auden, 1988.

Steenmeijer, Anne G. *A Tribute to Anne Frank.* New York: Doubleday, 1971.

Stein, André. *Quiet Heroes: True Stories of the Rescue of Jews by Christians in Nazi-Occupied Holland.* New York: New York University Press, 1988.

Tames, R. *Anne Frank.* New York: Franklin Watts, 1989.

van der Rol, Ruud, and Rian Verhoeven. *Anne Frank: Beyond the Diary,* trans. Tony Langham and Plym Peters. New York: Puffin Books, 1995.

van Galen Last, Dick, and Rolf Wolfswinkel. *Anne Frank and After: Dutch Holocaust Literature in Historical Perspective.* Amsterdam: Amsterdam University Press, 1996.

Yahil, Leni. *The Holocaust: The Fate of European Jewry,* trans. Ina Freidman and Haya Galai. New York: Oxford University Press, 1987.

Selected Videography

Anne Frank Remembered. Produced and directed by Jon Blair. 117 min. Columbia TriStar Home Video, 1996. 1996 Academy Award–winning documentary film about Anne Frank, includes interviews with people who knew her.

The Camera of My Family: Four Generations in Germany 1845–1945. 20 min. Zenger Video, 1991. Rise of Hitler and the Nazis in Germany as told through the memories and old photographs of one German Jewish family.

Camp of Hope and Despair: Westerbork Concentration Camp, 1939–1945 Produced and directed by Willy Lindwer. 70 min. Ergo Media, Inc. Through the eyewitness accounts of survivors, as well as remarkable photographs and films, we come to understand the overall picture of daily life in Westerbork.

The Courage to Care. Produced and directed by Robert Gardner. 28 min. PBS Video. Documentary film about ordinary people who rescued Jews during the Holocaust, includes a Dutch woman.

Dear Kitty. Produced and directed by Wouter van der Sluis. 29 min. Amsterdam Anne Frank Center. Anne Frank's life situated in a historical context and told through diary excerpts and photographs.

The Hangman. 12 min. CRM. An animated film of the Maurice Ogden poem in which a town watches as a mysterious sinister stranger hangs many of its inhabitants, one by one, without intervening.

The Last Seven Months: Women Search for Anne Frank. Produced and directed by Willy Lindwer. 75 min. Ergo Media, Inc. Moving documentary that begins where Anne Frank's diary leaves off. Previously unknown heartbreaking details about the final months and days of Anne's life.

The Diary of Anne Frank. Produced and directed by George Stevens. 151 min. CBS Fox Video, 1995. B & W film version of the Albert Hackett play; tells the story of Anne Frank's life in hiding. Originally released in 1959.

Triumph of Memory. Produced and directed by Robert Gardner. 28 min. PBS Video. A documentary film about four non-Jewish survivors of Mauthausen, Buchenwald, and Auschwitz-Birkenau concentration camps.

The World of Anne Frank. Produced and directed by Rob Weiner. 28 min. Ergo Media Inc. A film that tells Anne Frank's story by alternating between dramatization of her life and historical narration.

Selected Teaching Resources

Botwinick, Rita Steinhardt. *A History of the Holocaust: From Ideology to Annihilation.* Upper Saddle River, NJ: Prentice Hall, 1996.

Facing History and Ourselves: Holocaust and Human Behavior: Resource Book. Brookline, MA: Facing History and Ourselves National Foundation, 1995.

Gilbert, Martin. *Atlas of the Holocaust.* New York: Pergamon Press, 1988.

Grobman, Alex, Ph.D., and Joel Fishman, Ph.D. *Anne Frank in Historical Perspective: A   Teaching Guide for Secondary Schools.* Los Angeles: Martyrs Memorial and Museum of the Holocaust of the Jewish Federation, 1995.

Merti, Betty. *The World of Anne Frank: Readings, Activities, and Resources.* Portland, ME: J. Weston Walch, 1984.

Reader's Companion to Anne Frank: The Diary of a Young Girl. The Definitive Edition. New York: Doubleday, 1995.

A Resource Book for Educators: Teaching about the Holocaust. Washington, DC: United States Holocaust Memorial Museum, 1995.

Shawn, Karen. *The End of Innocence: Anne Frank and the Holocaust.* New York: Braun Center for Holocaust Studies, 1994. 2nd ed.

Wigoder, Geoffrey, ed. *The Holocaust: A Grolier Student Library.* 4 vols. Danbury, CT: Grolier Educational, 1997.

Contributors

Victoria J. Barnett, author of *For the Soul of the People: Protestant Protest Against Hitler* (New York: Oxford University Press, 1992), is a scholar who lives in Arlington, Virginia. Her articles have appeared in *The Christian Century* and *The Witness*. She is at work on a study of bystanders in the Holocaust.

Sidney Bolkosky is professor of history in the Honors Program at the University of Michigan–Dearborn. He co-authored, with Betty Rotberg Elias and David Harris, the Holocaust curriculum, *Life Unworthy of Life* (New York and Chicago: Glencoe Press, 1986). Dr. Bolkosky works extensively with Holocaust survivors in Detroit, Michigan.

G. Jan Colijn, dean of General Studies at The Richard Stockton College of New Jersey, has published numerous essays on the Holocaust. He also is the co-editor of several books, including, (with Marcia S. Littell), *The Netherlands and Nazi Genocide* (Lewiston, NY: Edwin Mellon Press, 1992).

Albert H. Friedlander is rabbi of Westminster Synagogue and dean of the Leo Baeck College, London, England. Many of his works deal with the Holocaust, notably, *Out of the Whirlwind: A Reader of Holocaust Literature* (New York: Schocken, 1976). He co-authored (with Elie Wiesel),

121

The Six Days of Destruction: Meditations toward Hope (New York: Paulist Press, 1988). Rabbi Friedlander has lectured at many universities in Europe and the United States.

Leo Goldberger is professor of psychology at New York University. He spent his early years in Denmark and was one of the Jews rescued in 1943 and taken to safety in Sweden. Dr. Goldberger is the editor of *Rescue of the Danish Jews: Moral Courage under Stress* (New York: New York University Press, 1987). He also has written several essays on the Danish rescue.

Patrick Henry teaches French at Whitman College in Walla Walla, Washington. He has published books on Voltaire, Montaigne, and *La Princesse de Cleves*. He also co-edits the journal *Philosophy and Literature*. Dr. Henry currently is doing research on the village of Le Chambon-sur-Lignon and the rescuers of Jews during the Holocaust.

Albert Hunt is a freelance journalist, documentary filmmaker, and author who has written on a variety of subjects for newspapers in England, Ireland, and other countries. Mr. Hunt has been involved in radical theater and drama for a number of years. He lives in Halifax, England.

Henry R. Huttenbach, editor of *The Genocide Forum (A Platform for Post-Holocaust Commentary)*, is professor of history at the City College of the City University of New York. He is the author of several books and articles on the Holocaust and genocide in general, including *The Destruction of the Jews of Worms, 1933–1975*.

Mary Johnson, a historian, is a program associate at the Facing History and Ourselves Foundation, Brookline, Massachusetts. Author of *Elements of Time* (Brookline, MA: FHAO, 1989), Dr. Johnson lectures extensively about the Holocaust for the Facing History Foundation. She gives workshops on how to teach about the Holocaust to teachers engaged in all levels of education.

Carol Rittner, the editor of *Anne Frank in the World,* is a Sister of Mercy from the Dallas, Pennsylvania Regional Community. She was appointed Ida E. King Distinguished Visiting Scholar of Holocaust Studies at The Richard Stockton College of New Jersey for 1994–1995, where she continues to teach as Distinguished Professor of Religion. In addition to her many Holocaust-related publications, Dr. Rittner was the executive producer for two films, *Triumph of Memory,* which is about non-Jews who survived Nazi concentration camps, and *The Courage to Care,* which is about rescuers of Jews during the Holocaust. The latter received a 1986 Academy Award nomination in the Short Documentary Film category.

John K. Roth is Russell K. Pitzer Professor of Philosophy, Claremont McKenna College. He has published more than twenty books and hundreds of articles, many of them focused on the Holocaust. A member of the United States Holocaust Memorial Council, Dr. Roth is also the author of the text for the permanent exhibition at the Holocaust Museum in Houston, which opened in that Texas city in 1996. With Carol Rittner, he co-edited *Different Voices: Women and the Holocaust* (New York: Paragon House, 1993).

Dorothee Söelle is an internationally known writer, scholar, and German Protestant Christian theologian. Born in Germany, where she still lives, Dr. Söelle has taught in Germany and in universities around the world, including Union Theologian Seminary in New York City. Among her many books are *The Strength of the Weak: Toward a Christian Feminist Identity* (Philadelphia: Westminster Press, 1984), and *Stations of the Cross: A Latin American Pilgrimage* (Minneapolis: Fortress Press, 1993).

Index

Ackroyd, Barry, 89
  voice of survivors, 89
Adenauer era, 41–42
Allies
  pilots, xxvii
Altruism, 72
Anne Frank
  and Helen Lewis, 21–22
battle against evil, 18
  belief in goodness, 6, 92
  child-author, 81
  child-victim, 82, 99
  courage, 65
    symbol of, 64–65
  cult figure of Holocaust studies,
    80
  distortions of Anne, 80–81
  essentials about, 81
  Holocaust child-hero, 79
  hope, 64
  human dimensions, 80
  idealism, 3, 6, 7–8, 64
  Jewish, 98–99
  optimism, 59, 64, 100–101
    misplaced, 100–101
  martyr, 100
  Peter Pan syndrome," 11
  problematic sentimentality, 78
  protesting affirmation, 78
  questions, 107
  teenagers today, 15
  transformed from a symbol, 90
"Anne Frank: A History for Today"
    (exhibit), 102–103
Anne Frank Center, 90

Anne Frank Foundation, 12, 79, 90
  work of, 12
Anne Frank House, Amsterdam, 15,
    79
"Anne Frank in the World 1929–
    1945" (exhibition), xii, xiii, 12–
    13, 14, 19–20, 35, 90–91, 97,
    105–106, 108, 113, 116
  Coventry Cathedral, 13
  Ken Livingston, 12
  St. Alban's Cathedral, 14
  themes, 106
    discrimination continues today,
      114–116
    discrimination is a matter of per-
      sonal choice, 113–114
    discrimination is cruel and irratio-
      nal, 109–111
    ordinary people discriminate,
      112–113
    society and the individual, 108–
      109
    who is Anne Frank?,
      106–108
Antisemitism, 23, 26, 96
Anschluss, xvii
Aristotle, 65–66
  emotions, 65–66
Arrendt, Hannah, *Eichman in Jeru-
    salem,* 99
Aryanization, xx
Aryan race, 23
Asocials, xxviii
Astrologers, xviii
Atrocities, 98

Auschwitz, xix, xx, xxi, xxii, xxiii, xxiv, xxvi, xxvii, xxviii, xxix, 21, 29–30, 60, 77, 90 91, 92, 107, 108, 111. *See also* Birkenau; Oswiecim
and God, 31. 32
crematoriums, xxix
liberation, 39
living after, 45
prisoners tattooed, 30–31
remaining human, 31
"selection," 32, 47
sonderkommando revolt, xxix
women in, 32
Austria, xvii, xx

Balen, Ivana, 56
Battle of Britain ("the blitz"), xix
Bauer, Yehuda, ix, x
BBC, 20, 50, 55
Belgrade (Yugoslavia), 56
Belgium, xix
Bergen-Belsen, xii, xxv, xxix, xxx, 5, 9, 21, 64, 78, 90, 92, 93, 107, 116
as memorial to Holocaust, 5–6
liberation of, xxx, 5
Berger, Joseph, 87
Berke, Jacqueline, 101
Beyond Hate: Living with Our Deepest Differences (conference), 19, 53, 56, 74
Beyond the Diary: Anne Frank in the World, xii
Birkenau, xx, xxiv, xxvii, xxviii. *See also* Auschwitz
Czech family camp, 30, 31–32

Blair, Jon, 88–90, 91, 92, 93
Anne Frank Remembered (film), 89, 91–92, 98–100
Schindler (film), 88
Block, Gay, 60, 61
Bohme, Jakob, 48
Bosnia, 22, 97–98
Bourgeois, 45, 76. *See also* Culture
German, 43
Bradford (England), 49
Bravery, 63–64
Bultmann, Rudolf, 44, 45, 46
Burning of books, xv
Bystanders, 96, 114. *See also* Non-resistance; "Fellow-travelers"

Cambodia, 97
Carnival for St. Valentine's Eve, A, 49. *See also* Dresden, fire-bombing

Challenge of the exception, xi
Chanukah, 11
Children, 16, 17, 90
and Holocaust diaries, 16–17
Moshe Flinker, 16
Jerzyk Urman, 16
and mothers, xxv
Jewish, xxi, 82–83
and Anne Frank, 82–83
Choice(s), 109, 113
Christianity, 43, 50, 100–101
"good" Christians, 101–102
Christian-Jewish dichotomy, 101–102
in play and diary, 101–102
Chris (Hunt), 49–50
Church leaders,xviii, xxvi
Collins, Alice, 75
Communists, 76
Concentration camps, 41

Concentration camps *(continued)*
Buchenwald, xvii, xxviii, 52
liberation of, xxx
Dachau, xv
liberation, 33, 39
Majdanek, xxvi, xxviii, 52–54, 60
Mauthausen, xx, xxi, xxiii, xxx
Neuengamme, xxix
Ravensbruck, xxviii
Sachsenhausen, xxii
Sobibor, xxii, xxiv, xxv
Stutthof, xviii, 22, 33
Terezin, 28–29, 30, 32. *See also*
Theresienstadt
Theresienstadt, 28–29, 70
Treblinka, xxiii
Westerbork, xviii, xxii, xxiii, xxiv,
xxvi, xxvii, xxviii, xxix, 91,
107
relationships in, 33
women in 32–33
Condor Legion, 53, 55
Courage, 63–64, 65, 67, 70–71, 72
acts of, 72
definition, 65
Courage to Care, The, 97
Marion Pritchard, 97
Croatia, 22
Culture, 43
German bourgeois, 43
relationship to Christianity, 43
Czechoslovakia, xvii, 21, 25, 26
Lidice, xxii
Nazi persecution, 26–27
Prague, 25–26, 28
Trutnov, 21, 26

D-Day, xxviii
Daily Telegraph (England), 54
Deane, Eamonn, 56
Death march 33–34

Dehistoricize and dejudaize, 98, 99
Denial, 40–41
Denmark, xix, xxvi, xxvii, 63, 68–
72
antisemitism, 68
Copenhagen, xxvi
Jews, xxvii
King Christian X, 69
Lutheran bishops, xxvii
rescue of Jews, 69–70
Deportation
of Danish Jews, xxvi
of Dutch Jews, xix, xx, xxi, xxii,
xxiii, xxv, xxvii
Despair, 24, 55, 56, 78
refusal to, 24
Die endlösung ("final solution"), x
Doneson, Judith, 100, 101
Doyle, Aidan, 52
Dresden (Germany), 53, 54, 55, 57
corpse-mines, 51
fire-bombing, xxx, 49–51
firestorm, 51, 53
Drucker, Malka, 60–61
Duckwitz, Georg, xxvi
Dussel, Albert, xxiii, 58. *See also*
Pfeffer, Fritz
Dusseldorf (Germany), 57
Dutch elites, 96
moral responsibility, 96
Dutch Nazi sympathizers, 98
Dutch universities, xxi
Dylan, Bob, 55

East Germany, 49–50
Education, 97–98. *See also* Holocaust and teaching
goal, 97
critical goal of 97
teaching about *The Diary of
Anne Frank,* 102–103

Einsatzgruppen (killing squads), xx
Eisenhower, Dwight W., xxviii
Elff, Jeanne, xiv
"Enemies of the state," 113. *See also
Untermenschen* (subhumans)
England
  Coventry, 52
  London, 52–53, 54
En-sof of God, 17
Ephimenco, Sylvain, 95
Eternal Jew, The, (film), 98
Ethnic cleansing, 23, 56, 73, 75, 78,
  111, 114
Euthanasia program, xviii. *See also* T-
  4
Evian conference, xvii
Evil, 30, 55, 56, 72

Fear, 65, 70
"Fellow-traveler," 39–40. See also
  Bystander; Non-resistance
Ferrie, Liam, 74–75
  The Irish Emigrant, 74–75
Final Solution, xxi, xxii, xxviii, 75,
  78, 110. See also *Die
  endlösung*
Fogelman, Eva, 60, 61
Forgiveness, 45
Fortune tellers, xviii
France, xviii, xix
  Paris, xix
  Vichy, xix
Frank family
  Jews, 108
Frank, Otto, ix, x, xvii, xix, xx,
  xxix, xxx, xxxi, 9, 10–11, 13,
  15, 79, 81, 108
  becomes a legend, 12
  and Fritzi, 12
  Joseph Schildkraut, 12
Frankfurt am Main (Germany), xv

Freud, Sigmund, *Civilization and Its
  Discontents,* 76, 77
Genocide, 82
German
  army, 34
  fascism, 42
Germany, xviii, xix, xx, xxi, xxiii,
  xxiv, 22, 25
  Munich, xv
  Wannsee, 110
Gestapo, xxvi, xxviii, 70
Gies, Jan, ix, xi
Gies, Miep, ix, xi, 81–82, 89, 93, 96,
  101, 102, 108. *See also* Helpers;
  Rescuers; Righteous gentiles
God, 48
Goebbels, Joseph, xvii, 76
Goethe, 43
Goldhagen, Daniel, *Hitler's Willing
  Executioners: Ordinary Ger-
  mans and the Holocaust,* 95–96
Goodness, 8
Goodrich, Frances and Albert
  Hackett, *The Diary of Anne
  Frank,* 14
Göring, Herman, xxi
Goslar, Hannah ("Lies"), 98,
  99. *See also* Pick, Hannah
Grass, Gunter, *The Tin Drum,* 40
Great Britain, xviii, xxi
Great depression, xv
Guernica (Spain), 55
Guilt, 44–45. *See also* Sin
  Anne's sense of, 58
Gypsy (-ies), xviii, xxiv, xxviii
  in Auschwitz-Birkenau, xxviii

Hamburg (Germany), 53, 54
"Hardy" people, 67
  characteristics of, 67
  non-hardy person, 67

Hardiness Test Questionnaire, 67
Hate, 77
Hegarty, Mary Christopher, xiii, 20
Heidigger (Martin), 40
Helper(s), 101, 114, 115. *See also*
    Rescuers; Righteous gentiles
Herd instinct, 72–73
    tribalism, 73
Hermann, Hajo, 53–54
Het Achterhuis (The Secret Annex),
    xxx
Heydrich, Reinhard, xxi, xxii, 28
Hillesum, Etty, xxvi
Himmler, Heinrich, xviii, xix, xx, xxiv
Historiography, 96
Hitler, Adolf, xv, xviii, xxx, 39, 42–
    43, 76
    assassination attempt, xxviii
    Mein Kampf, 110
    suicide, xxx
Hitler Youth, 40, 57
Holland, xviii, xix, xxi, xxii, xxiii,
    xxv, xxvi, xxvii xxviii, 40,
    72, 97, 109, 111. *See also*
    Netherlands
    Amsterdam, xix, xx, xxii, xxiv, xxv
    Anne Frank's house, 52
    general strike, xx
    Jews, xxiv
    antisemitic legislation, 111
    Assen, xviii
    protest strikes, xxv
    Rotterdam, 52
    The Hague, xxiv
Holocaust, ix, x, 75
    abandonment of idealism, 6–7
    and evil, 7, 23–24
    and idealism after, 23–24
    education about mandated, 102
    how it should be remembered, 5–6
    remembrance, 22

Holocaust *(continued)*
    survivors 20 , 92
    teaching, x–xi, 87, 97
    curricula, 88
    educational goals, 92–93, 97
    materials, 87–88
    world of, world after, 16
Hope, 45, 64
Huguenots (Protestants), xvi
Human nature, 8
    destructive urge, 59
Human rights, 114
Hungary, xxviii
Hunger, 29

IRA (Irish Republican Army), 75
Iraq, 55
Italy, xxi

Japan, xxi
    Hiroshima, xxx, 49, 53, 57
    Nagasaki, xxx, 53
Jehovah's Witnesses, xvii
Jewish
    council, xx. See also *Joodse Raad;*
        Judenrat
    passivity, 59
    rescuers of Jews, 59
    resistance, xx
    star, xxiii. *See also* Yellow star;
        Star of David
Jewish tradition, 47
Joodse Raad, xx
Judaism, 8
Judenrat, xx
    newspaper, xxiii
Juden verboten (No Jews), xvi
Judgment at Nuremberg (film), 7

Kaddish, 17
Kirchentag, 44

Kitty (Anne's diary), 58, 82, 107
  Anne's confidences, 82
Kleiman, Johannes, ix, x, xi
Kogon, Eugen, *The SS-State,* 41
Kray, Susan, 101
Kristallnacht, xvii
Kugler, Victor, ix, x, xi

Language, 46
  Irish, 52
Law for the Prevention of Hereditar-
  ily Diseased Offspring, xv
League of German Maidens, 40
Lebensunwertes leben (lives unwor-
  thy of life), xvi
Le Chambon-sur-Lignon (France),
  xvi, xix, xxvi, 59–60
  "House of Rocks," xxvi
  liberated by French troops,
    xxix
Levi, Primo, 93
Levin, Meyer
  dramatic version of *The Diary of
    Anne Frank,* 13–14
  encounter with Otto Frank, 14
Lewis, Harry, 34, 35
Lewitt, Maria, 50
Life Unworthy of Life project, 87.
Lindwer, Willy, *The Last Seven
    Months of Anne Frank* (film),
  102
Luther (Martin), 40
Luxemburg, xix

Mandela, Nelson, 97
Melchior, Marcus, xxvi
Memory, 48, 54, 61. *See also* Re-
  membrance
Milca Mayerova's School of Dance,
  25
Miller, Judith, 95

Minco, Marga, *Bitter Herbs: A Little
    Chronicle,* 102
Mixed marriages, xxv, xxvi–xxvii
Models of human behavior, xi
Montessori (school), xvi
Moral virtues, 65
Mullan, Deirdre (Sister), xiii, 20
Munich conference, xvii
Mussert, Anton, 108

National Socialism, 42
National Socialist Party (Nazis), xv
Nazis, 42
  boycott, xv
  era, 42
  indoctrinating youth, 112
Nazism
  rise of, 109–110
Netherlands, xix, xx. *See also* Hol-
    land
  nazi support in, 97
  war against the Jews, 99
Netherlands State Institute, 10
New Testament, 11
Niemoeller, Martin, 115
Nightmares, 35
Non-Jews, xxii
  Poles, xxiv
Non-resistance, 39–40. *See also* By-
    stander
Northern Ireland, xii, 19–20, 22, 35,
  53, 74
  Belfast, 34
  Derry, 74–75
  Thornhill College, xii, xiii, 20,
    35
Norway, xix
Nuremberg Laws, xvi
  Law for the Protection of German
    Blood and Honor, xvi
  Reich Citizenship Law, xvi

"Operation Market Garden," xxix
Opekta-Works Company, xvi, xx.
   See also Trading Company
   Gies & Company
Orwell, George, 54
Oswiecim, xix. *See also* Auschwitz

Palestinians, 57
"Peace in our time," 26
Pearl Harbor, xxi
Pectacon B. V., xvii
Peron, Evita, 99
Perpetrators, 114, 115
Pfeffer, Fritz, ix, xiii. *See also*
   Dussel, Albert
Pforzheim (Germany), 51–52, 53,
   54–55
Pick, Hannah, 100. *See also* Goslar,
   Hannah ("Lies")
Poland, xviii, xix, xx, xxii, xxiv,
   xxvi, 50
   German-occupied, 111
   Lublin, 52, 111
   Lvov, 111
   Warsaw, xviii, 111
   ghetto, xxiv, 52 , 111
   uprising, xxiv
*Political theologyA Debate with
   Rudolf Bultmann,* 44
Post-Holocaust, 60
Post-traumatic stress,
   34–35
Prayer, 47–48
Presser, Jacob, *The Destruction of
   the Dutch Jews,* 97, 102
Prisoners
   Jewish, xxv
   political, xxii
   POWs
      Dutch, xxv
      Soviet, xxi, xxv

Propaganda
   anti-nazi, 52–53
   nazi, 112
Protocols of the Elders of Zion, The,
   23
Psychology, 65–66
   abstractions, 65
   displacement and projection, 66–
      67
   fight-flight mechanism, 66–67
   scapegoating, 66–67

Questions, 40–41, 46, 47, 60, 61,
   75, 97, 109, 110, 111, 112–
   113, 113–114, 115–116
   about Anne Frank, 79–80
   German question, 45
   Teaching, 87
   Theological, 44

"Race science," 112
RAF Bomber Command, 49, 51
Red Cross, 70
Refugees, xxvii
Reichstag, xvii
Relationship between Jews and non-
   Jews, 24–25
Religion, 42
Remembrance, 57. *See also* Mem-
   ory
Rescue, 107–108
Rescuers. *See also* Righteous gen-
   tiles
   characteristics of, 60–61, 71
   Danish, 71–72
   Dutch, 71
   Essential principles, 61
   French, 71
   Personal responsibility, 61
Resistance
   Danish, xxvi, xxvii

Resistance *(continued)*
  Dutch, xxiv, 96
  German student, xxiv
  Jewish, 59
  women, 56
Revisionists, 54
Righteous gentiles, 63, 71–72,
  96. *See also* Rescuers; Helpers
  in Holland, 97
  demythologize "good" Dutch, 97
Roosevelt, President (Franklin D.),
  xxi
Rosenfeld, Alvin, 100, 101
Rosh Hashanah, 69
Rwanda, 97

Sabra and Shatila (Lebanon), 54, 57
Scholl, Sophie and Hans, xxiv, 108–
  109
  White Rose, xxiv
Schindler, Oskar, 93
Schuler, Georgette, 3, 4, 7, 9
Secret annex, ix, x, xxii, xxiii, 59,
  91, 93, 106–107
Sectarian violence, 75, 78
Seyss-Inquart, Artur, xxv
Shame, 32–33, 40, 41, 47
  Anne's sense of, 58
  collective, 40
Shoah, 39, 48, 75. *See also* Holocaust
Silberbauer, Karl Josef, ix, xi
Sin, 44–45. *See also* Guilt
*Six Days of Destruction, Medita-
  tions Towards Hope, The,* 17
Sonderbahandlung (special treat-
  ment), 31
Soviet Union, xx, 22
Spielberg, Steven, 87
  Schindler's List (film), 87, 93
"St. Matthew's Passion," 47
St. Valentine's Eve, 49, 50

Star of David, 27, 72. *See also* Yel-
  low star; Jewish star
Sterilization, xvi, xxv
  in mixed marriages, xxv
Stevens, George, 90
Stockton College, 100
Stories, 56, 57
Students
  Dutch, xxv
  German anti-nazi xxiv
Sturmabteilung, 76
Sudeten territories, xvii, 26
Sweden, xxvii, 71

T-4 program, xviii. *See also* Eutha-
  nasia, program, xviii
Theology, 43
  liberation, 46
  political, 44
  post-Auschwitz, 41
Tiananmen Square, 63–64
Time to Speak, A, 20, 21, 22
Tikkun olam, xii
Trading Company Gies & Com-
  pany, xx. *See also* Opekta-
  Works
Trocmé, Andre, xvi
Trocmé, Daniel, xxvi, xxviii, 59–60,
  61
Trocmé, Magda, xvi, xix

United Churches of the Netherlands,
  xxv
United Fruit Company, 44
United States, xxi
Untermenschen (subhuman), 113
Unworthiness
  Anne's sense of, 58

V-E day, xxx
V-J day, xxx

van Daans, ix, xxiii. *See also* van
     Pels
van der Zee, Nanda, 96–97
van Pels. *See also* van Daans
     Auguste, ix, xxii, xxix, xxx
     Hermann, ix, xxix
     Peter, ix, xxix, xxx
Victims, 115
Vietnam war, 44
von Ribbentrop, xxiii
von Rath, Ernst, xvii
von Schirach, Baldur, 108
Vonnegut, Kurt, *Slaughterhouse
     Five,* 51
Voskuilj, Elizabeth ("Bep"), ix, xi

Wagner (Richard), 40
Wannsee conference, xxi
Warmbrunn, Werner, *The Dutch
     Under German Occupation,
     1940–1945,* 102

Weimar Republic, xv, 22
Wessel, Horst, 75–76, 77
     "Horst Wessel Song," 76, 78
     "Raise High the Flag" (poem),
          76
Westminster Synagogue, 13
Wiesel, Elie, 17, 46, 47, 89–90, 92
     Night, 89, 92
Wine of remembrance, 54, 55,
     56
Woollams, Erika, 50–51, 57
Women, 32–33
     Dutch, 102
     German, xxiv

Yellow star, xx, xxii, 27. *See also*
     Jewish star; Star of David

Zachor, 17
Zigeunerlager (Gypsy camp), xxiv
Zyklon B, xxi, 41, 47